Trusting the
Moment

If experience is the best teacher, then Jeannie Lindheim is the next best thing — a teacher who has created 50 powerful experiences that help people learn how to be fully alive, compassionate, courageous, creative human beings. This book is a goldmine of ideas for anyone interested in the burgeoning field of experiential education. I recommend it enthusiastically!
    — **Richard Borofsky, EdD, Clinical psychologist, Co-founder of the Center for the Study of Relationship**

Cultivating spontaneity is the key to the development of the capacity to be really adaptive in a time of increasing changes. This book offers practical techniques for acquiring the skills of creativity and flexibility.
    — **Adam Blatner, MD, retired psychiatrist, author, *Acting-In: Practical Applications of Psychodramatic Methods***

This well organized book can help you facilitate groups with a wide variety of stimulating new ideas and exercises to awaken self-awareness and creativity. Jeannie Lindheim comes from a theater background with experience in offering challenging and meaningful improvisations. She has also written about the art of group leadership, which is the most important part of facilitating any group. Using movement, art, journal writing and improvisation integrates all of the senses as this book suggests.
    — **Natalie Rogers, PhD, psychologist and author of *The Creative Connection: Expressive Art as Healing***

This is a go-to guide for exercises that facilitate relationships through meaningful — and what we are now forced to call "live" or "real-time" — human interaction. Jeannie's activities constitute an ethics of group bonding by harmonizing the heart of the individual with the soul of the community.
    — **Daniel Spector, Director, Drama Instructor, Tisch School of the Arts at NYU**

Jeannie has done a wonderful job . . . of making accessible to any group or organization a treasure trove of exercises culled from her years of experience as an acting teacher. She teaches people how to lead each exercise successfully and lays out what problems to be aware of. This book would be particularly useful for teachers, directors, and leaders in any situation that involves group dynamics. She teaches you how to lead, and has tips for people who are just starting out, as well as advanced exercises for serious professionals interested in doing advanced work.
    — **Davis Robinson, Professor of Theater, Bowdoin College**

Jeannie has such an impressive wealth of knowledge and ideas! The exercises are a goldmine. Her voice and passion about this work comes through so powerfully! What I found valuable were the suggestions for alternative ways to conduct an exercise, what to expect in some cases and how to handle difficult situations.
    — **Ilana Traverse, Instructional Designer and Facilitator, Principal of IMA Associates**

Jeannie Lindheim's handbook gives you lifetimes of her invaluable insights. You'll learn how to creatively inspire people to see new ways of being — and seeing — what's possible for themselves and for others. The book has three lifetimes of invaluable experiences or more.
    — **Nance Guilmartin, author, *The Power of Pause: How to Be More Effective in a Demanding 24/7 World* and *Healing Conversations: What to Say When You Don't Know What to Say***

Fantastic information and exercises. This book is great for coaches because a lot of exercises help us to get other perspectives or in touch with secret/hidden aspects of ourselves. Trusting the Moment is so very full of great ideas and wisdom. I am inspired.
    — **Christine Thomas, CPCC, ORSCC, Certified Life and Relationship Coach**

Trusting the Moment

Unlocking Your Creativity and Imagination

A handbook for individual and group work,
including fifty exercises to increase cohesiveness and creativity

JEANNIE LINDHEIM, MFA

SATYA HOUSE PUBLICATIONS
Hardwick, Massachusetts

First Edition
Printed in Canada

ISBN 978-1-9358740-0-3 (paperback edition)

Publisher's Cataloging-In-Publication Data
(*Prepared by The Donohue Group, Inc.*)

Lindheim, Jeannie.
  Trusting the moment : unlocking your creativity and imagination / Jeannie Lindheim. — 1st ed.

    p. ; cm.

  "A handbook for individuals and people who work creatively with others, including fifty exercises to increase cohesiveness and creativity."
  Includes bibliographical references.
  ISBN: 978-1-935874-00-3 (pbk.)

  1. Creative thinking—Problems, exercises, etc. 2. Creative ability—Problems, exercises, etc. 3. Imagination—Problems, exercises, etc. 4. Cooperativeness. 5. Social groups. I. Title.

BF408 .L56 2011
153.3/5   2010940673

This publication is available at special discounts for bulk purchases for educational needs. Customizing options are available upon request. For details, write Satya House Special Markets, P. O. Box 122, Hardwick, MA 01037

Satya House Publications
P. O. Box 122
Hardwick, Massachusetts 01037
orders@satyahouse.com § www.satyahouse.com

To my sweet, wonderful, inspirational man, Steven

Acknowlegements

How do you thank everyone in your life who inspired you to be creative?

To my sixty-three stuffed animals who grounded me when I was a little girl. We had 'meetings' every Sunday night. I had a different voice for each animal and we discussed important issues of the day. Panda, the President, to this day sits in our living room.

Mr. Strater, my 8th grade drama teacher, who walks into class one day and falls in a heap on the floor. He gets up and says, "We are going to learn how to fall today." And I know, this is what I want to do with my life . . . be creative and have fun.

To the auditioners at Boston University who let me into the theater department. My audition is from Lillian Hellman's *The Little Foxes*. The character is Birdie, a 50-year-old alcoholic. At the audition, I am 18-years-old. I look 12, wearing bobby socks and brown and white saddle shoes. They probably needed to take someone in the program from Ohio because my audition must have been terrible.

Tom Yeomans, my spiritual coach and friend. Morrie Schwartz, who let me visit him during the last eight months of his life. Morrie was never dying, he was always living. His humor, grace and vulnerability touched my soul. Olivia Hoblitzelle, for her wisdom and gentleness. Tom, Morrie and Olivia are true role models for me.

The magical state of Vermont for her beauty, peace and inspiration. Vermont thrills, gentles and heals me.

Jeanne Carbonetti, a gifted watercolorist and magnificent teacher who lets me fly with my paints.

All of the dance teachers who let me come four times a week to class and stand in the back of the room, to learn the routines that most students learn in one class.

Uta Hagen and Stephen Strimpell, two brilliant acting teachers.

All of the directors who took a chance in casting me in shows.

The authors listed on my Personal Growth List. Books are some of my most precious teachers.

Cheryl Lekousi, who took over the leadership of the Hearts and Noses Hospital Clown Troupe, so I could realize other dreams, and for holding our dream of the troupe so it continues on.

To the amazing children in the hospital with whom we visit. We let the child control the hospital clown. The children inspire our creativity.

Peggy Martin and Maureen Mondor, for trusting me to create and lead the workshops for physicians.

Richard Gonzales, a caring Afro-Caribbean dance teacher. He gave me my center back in movement, after I had breast cancer, and had no center at all.

Susan Troyan, MD, a kind and wonderful surgeon. The last thing I remember during my last surgery was looking toward the operating room and seeing her wearing the red clown nose I gave her a few moments before.

Chris Wisniewski, one of the most creative website designers in the universe. Ruth Harriet Jacobs, whose words are priceless. Patricia Ryan Madson, who shared her experience and supported me along the way. Elana Rosenbaum, for her kind advice; Nick Bissel, for adding stardust to my life; Liz Chinean, for her warmth and great work helping me.

Janelle Winston, the most amazing friend and Speech Coach in the world. A huge thanks to the people who read drafts of this book and made fabulous suggestions: Ken Baltin, Beth Davenport, Gary Genard, Nance Guilmartin, Bette Hoffman, Carolyn Holland, Joann Javons, Bill Lacey, Tammy Gooler Loeb, Christine Thomas, Ilana Traverse, and Katherine Waters-Clark. To all these talented people, I am forever grateful. And a huge thanks to our fabulous proofreader, Cristy Bertini.

Martha Hennessy, who introduced me to Maidstone Lake, where the mystical loon calls leave me breathless. Catherine Bowdren, a dear creative friend who warms my heart.

To all the sweet animals I have known. They truly are my greatest teachers.

To fantasy land, a land I inhabit often. I could have gotten a PhD in daydreaming.

All of my incredibly creative students, who inspired me to be creative and take risks, even when they weren't so sure of what would happen. And neither was I.

My sweet gifted children, Josh and Julie, who lived with a mother who gave thirty-eight Perfect People Parties and saw crazy students coming in and out of our house all the time during these parties. They've put up with my wackiness and I love them for it. Raising them with their innocence, honesty and play was a delight.

Tinkerbell, the most affectionate magical cat in the world. She's always there, snuggles under the covers and her purrs are the best; and Snowy, our blue and white parakeet who sings most of the day and her wolf whistles always take me by surprise. She makes me smile. And JC (Julie's cat, Josh's cat, Jeannie's cat) you are always with me.

Julie Murkette, the most fabulous publisher/editor ever! Her patience, warmth, creativity and kindness are forever in my heart.

Steven, my sweet creative light in my life. His love makes me bold. His support makes me risk. His humor makes me laugh and his caring is the best.

Contents

Moment after moment we are creating something, and this is the joy of our life.
— Shunryu Suzuki, Zen Master

Foreword

My education was painful. It was competitive. It was based on grades, rather than the process of learning. Most teachers asked for regurgitation, not creativity. So, I found my haven in theater. It was fun. I was able to express all of the parts of me.

I'll never forget my first drama class in eighth grade with Mr. Strater. He is a large man and on the first day of class, he walks into the room and falls down as if he had died. I am shocked. Then he stands up and says, "Today we are going to learn how to fall on stage." It is now fifty years later and I have never forgotten that incredible moment. He created magic and surprise and I loved it.

Theater allows me to explore, risk and create. I went to college and majored in theater. It is my love. I trained as an actress. Although some of the acting classes are competitive, cutthroat and destructive, others are warm and supportive. I feel like I am part of a family. Acting in productions is wonderful. We are all working and creating together because we have a common goal. I find that the group process is just as important as the production itself. I enjoy the rehearsals more than the actual performance because in rehearsals we can risk, experiment and try anything.

Through my training as an actress and director, I learned to be vulnerable, to share, and most importantly for the purposes of this book, to create an ensemble. An ensemble is a group whose members have a deep connection to one another and to the work at hand. That's what is important to me in the work I do now, with actors, therapists, clergy, teachers, professional helpers and group leaders. That's why I form a circle at the first group meeting. The circle is a symbol of connection, unity and wholeness. These are the qualities I want to encourage and create in my groups.

My groups reflect how I believe life should be. The environment I try to create in the groups is the same kind of environment I want in my own life: creative, supportive and caring. I have found that in this kind of environment, attention is paid to the process and not to the results. The most important part about being an artist is becoming comfortable with the process of **creating** and **becoming**.

Besides my theater training, I have taken many kinds of workshops in psychology-psychodrama, transactional analysis, psychosynthesis, Gestalt and more. After each workshop, I took the crème de la crème of what I had learned in the group and applied it to my own teaching. The group leaders I have worked with were role models. They made each group experience a double learning experience. I learned about my own process and also how to be a group leader. I watched many leaders handle difficult and stressful situations.

As a group leader/teacher/acting coach, I help people bring out their 'sub-personalities' or different parts of themselves. To do this successfully, I must trust, risk and be comfortable with the unknown. The purpose of this book is to help others who work with groups gain confidence in these areas.

Several people have warned me that these exercises could be threatening to some group leaders. At first, this surprised me. But then I realized that people come from different training arenas. Many people are taught NOT to risk or express themselves freely. We are not taught to be vulnerable with other people. Instead, we are taught to be controlled, safe and predictable.

Working with a group, be it at a workshop, in a classroom or on a retreat, should be one of the most exciting learning experiences in the world, for the group leader as well as for the participants. But our educational system can be full of judgments. Many teachers tell us there is a right way to do something and a wrong way. Many students, as well as their teachers, are frozen. They are unable to be creative or inventive. We carry this experience with us into group situations and this blocks our spontaneity and creativity. I hope this book will help you remove the blocks to spontaneity and creativity for yourself and for the people who are in your groups.

Many colleges and universities have artist-in-residence programs. The point of these programs is to allow students and teachers to see professional artists at work. This can be exciting, but I believe it's far more exciting—and more important—for people to learn that **we are all artists**. For those of you who feel timid about trying out these techniques and exercises, I want to say to you, "Go slowly. Be gentle with yourself and your groups." *Trusting the Moment* means trusting the process, and most importantly, trusting yourself. You will be amazed at the excitement and joy you and your groups will experience—together. I love something a student of mine wrote in his journal when I asked him to explain what he thought teaching was all about: "My philosophy of teaching is simple. I don't just want to teach that two plus two is four, but I want to teach that if one person has two and another person has two, **together** they have four." We all work together to create an ensemble.

People often write me and say, "I loved your group and the exercises, but the most wonderful thing about the group was that I learned so much about myself." In a journal I wrote in 1971, I said that one of my goals was to help change the educational system in this country. I haven't done that, and maybe I won't see any significant change during my lifetime. But, then again, maybe I will. If people come to understand themselves better, who knows what could happen? At least this is a beginning.

With love,
Jeannie Lindheim
Brookline, Massachusetts

Faith is to believe what we do not see;
the reward of this faith is to see what we believe.

— St. Augustine

Why This Book Is Valuable

The purpose of this book is to give you a set of tools that will make you a more effective, exciting and *excited* artist and/or group leader. It includes ideas on the art of group leadership, as well as specific suggestions for group procedures. The heart of the book includes fifty exercises that will:

- Break the ice when your group first meets
- Free people from the blocks and inhibitions that many people bring to one-on-one and to group situations
- Encourage your group members to be open, vulnerable and trusting with each other
- Build a warm and supportive environment, where each person will feel free to express his or her own creativity and joy
- Develop a bond between group members that will allow each one to be spontaneous and take risks

When you use the exercises in this book, you will help participants and/or yourself to:

- Build self esteem and confidence
- Get to know themselves in new and exciting ways
- Become more imaginative and sensitive to others
- Commit to new situations and follow through on impulses
- Take off their masks and express different parts of themselves
- Build memory, concentration and listening skills
- Become more comfortable with their bodies
- Learn to lead, as well as to follow
- Become more flexible, physically and emotionally
- Learn how to live in the moment
- Develop a greater sense of life possibilities that are open to them

These exercises combine movement, improvisation, guided imagery, symbolic drawing and other activities that open new doors. They require that you, and the members of your group, think on your feet because they demand spontaneity. The exercises will stretch you to your creative limits. Stereotypes and preconceptions will break down and empathy and compassion will grow. The environment you create by doing the exercises will let your group laugh and be silly together. There will be a freshness and excitement at each group meeting.

These exercises are excellent diagnostic tools for the group leader. By using these exercises, you will see how each person perceives him or herself. Since the exercises are open-ended, they are flexible enough to be useful for many types of people. Once you get to know the members of your group, you will be able to use the exercises to help each of them develop their own unique creativity.

Watching your group grow as they do the exercises is the most thrilling part of leading groups. This book will provide the tools you need so that you and your group can really soar **together**!

To summarize, this book tells you how to successfully introduce these exercises into your group, how to maintain group energy, and how to ground the experience of each exercise. And it teaches you how to be open and vulnerable yourself, how to be *in the process* along with your group, while maintaining just enough distance to keep control and create the needed safety within your group.

When you become open and vulnerable as a group leader, the way is paved for your group to share their most valuable and treasured parts of themselves. These exercises and tools will allow each person's creative fire to ignite!

Take life too seriously and what is it worth? If the morning wakes us to no new joys,
if the evening brings us not the hope of new pleasure, is it worthwhile to dress and undress?
— Johann Wolfgang von Goethe, German writer

Who This Book Is For

People in the helping professions love doing the exercises in my workshops and on retreats. The exercises open up their own creativity and they discover parts of themselves that have been hidden for years. Even though the exercises were originally designed for actors, they are helpful therapeutic tools. You can do them one-on-one with your clients and patients.

Teachers face the challenging task of having to come up with new material for students, day in and day out. These exercises can easily be adapted to many classroom situations. They can be used to teach language arts, social studies, math, sociology, psychology, history, art, music, theater and more. You can integrate these exercises into your curriculum. For example, improvisation can be based on historical situations and you will bring history into the present by role-playing. Your teaching becomes exciting and experiential for your students. Physicalizing what they are learning helps students experience their creativity in new and exciting ways. The possibilities are endless.

Youth leaders face challenges similar to those faced by teachers of all levels. Often, students are apathetic or downright resistant. I once taught at a school of high school dropouts. There were sixteen young men and it was rough. They fought me tooth and nail for about three weeks and then a transformation occurred. They began to love the material and the process. The trust took longer to develop within this group because basically, they didn't trust anyone. But once they did trust me, and each other, miracles began to happen.

People who work with a physically disabled population will find it challenging and exciting to try these exercises. Believe it or not, I taught movement and improvisation to people who are paraplegics and quadriplegics. Many in the group had speech difficulties. At first it was challenging for me to understand them, but after fifteen minutes, the wheelchairs were moving and we were all communicating with each other in amazing ways. The exercises were effective in bringing people out of themselves.

Senior citizens love the exercises. They play, are creative, and have fun. While teaching in a Senior Center, I was excited to see how brilliant many of the participants are. They were grateful to have the opportunity to take risks and go into new areas of creativity where they had never been before.

People who work with people on a one-on-one basis can use these techniques effectively. As you the read the Art of Group Leadership, you will see universal principles that apply to your work with just one client. The concepts, tools, and techniques will make your work with clients richer and more exciting. You will have more to draw on in your work with the people you see. **Coaches** can use these exercises with one client or with groups they facilitate. You can even do many of the exercises over the phone.

Writers, painters, dancers and other artists can do these exercises alone. Although creativity is wonderful when it is experienced in groups, it is just as rich when you create alone. You can open up and stimulate your creative juices with many of the techniques in this book.

The obvious audience for this book is **actors, directors, and acting teachers.** I have seen these exercises create marvelous transformations in the attitudes and work of thousands of actors and directors.

I believe that **people who work creatively with people** will gain a tremendous amount of joy from this book. The exercises, philosophy and tips for group leaders will give you the roots, foundation, and a feeling of safety so you can successfully introduce the exercises to your group.

Enjoy! You are about to go on a creative and exciting journey. . . .

I see my life as an unfolding set of opportunities to awaken.
— Ram Dass, spiritual teacher, writer

How To Use This Book

This book can be used two ways. You can either read it cover to cover or go right to an exercise that you might want to do with your group. The first part of the book provides ideas for successfully introducing the exercises to your group. You may already have this expertise.

In that case, you can scan the first part of the book and then go directly to the exercises. Or, you may want to intersperse reading the first part on leadership with the second part of the book, which are the exercises.

The first section of the book is called *The Art of Group Leadership.* There are suggestions on how you can be an even more dynamic and sensitive group leader. There are tips for leading the exercises, tips on leading your group, tips on how to handle problems, tips for coaching improvisations, and tips on how to take care of yourself as a group leader.

The second section of this book includes the exercises, which are the heart of the book.

I'd like to suggest ways that you might approach the exercises. One approach is that you read through **all** of the exercises. This will give you the flavor of the book. As you read them, you might want to take notes on the exercises that seem appropriate for the kinds of groups you lead. I've provided the *purpose* for each exercise, but by using your own creativity, you can come up with your own purposes for doing the exercises.

Depending on your time constraints, you can check Appendix F: Time Requirements for Each Exercise. The exercises range from ten minutes to ninety minutes each. Most of them can be adapted to fit into almost any time frame you have. You can read the exercise over and see what part of it fits into your group plan.

The Time Requirements are general. Most of the exercises have many parts. You can work with one part of an exercise. The longer exercises can be broken down into shorter exercises of 15-30 minutes. Some exercises, if done in their entirety, might take several hours.

It is helpful if you let each exercise percolate in your mind and body for a few days. As I created them, I allowed what I call *musing time.* Ideas came to mind, as I was washing the dishes or playing with our pet rabbit, on how I might best structure the exercise.

> **Please be aware that the part of the exercise under Procedure
> is written as if you were talking DIRECTLY to your group.**

This means that you can read over the exercise and then paraphrase it in a way that feels comfortable for you. The exercises are adaptable, open-ended and evolving. You are free to transform them and make them your own. You will find your own creativity flourishing!

The Appendices have suggestions for improvisational settings and situations, suggestions for two, three and more people improvisations, suggestions for character professions you can use in improvisations and questions to help your group come up with imaginary autobiographies of their characters. There is a section on personal growth books and wonderful theater books. You will also see the Time requirements for each exercise.

I want to encourage you to use this book in the way that works best for you. Let your intuition be your guide. You have my approach here, the exercises I love doing with groups. Distill from it what is most valuable for you. You can use the techniques and exercises just as they are presented. Or you can use them as stepping-stones toward creating your own exercises. If you don't feel comfortable with an entire exercise, you can use just a part of it.

However you use this book, if you are loving toward the people in your groups, these exercises will work. I have done all of the exercises for twenty-five years and I know they work.

I offer you a guarantee. These exercises and philosophy behind them will change your group. This work is all about experimenting, taking risks and bringing out new energy and creativity. I know that once you try a few of the exercises, you will want to do them all.

One last suggestion. Go slowly, be gentle with yourself and trust that you can make these exercises work beautifully with your group. I know you will!

The teacher of the actor is like the teacher of small children. He looks for the right steps for each student, and when the student is about to make his discovery, the teacher must disappear. If the teacher looks for his own satisfaction at the point of discovery, the student does not fully discover. Take a child who has a pile of blocks but can't find a way to make what he wants out of them. If the teacher guides him in making the shape the child wants to make, he should disappear when the child is about to take the definitive step. By taking this step himself, the child discovers his own thoughts.

— Joseph Chaiken, stage director, founder of the Open Theater

How The Exercises Are Organized

The exercises are divided into three sections: Beginning, Intermediate and Advanced. The criteria for differentiating between Beginning, Intermediate and Advanced are as follows:

Difficulty: How difficult the exercise is for the group to accomplish.
Trust: How much trust you need in your group to do the exercise.
Ensemble and Connection: How well your group needs to work together to perform the exercise.
Risk: How much risk the exercise involves.

All groups are different. You could find an exercise in the Intermediate or Advanced section that you might want to use as a Beginning exercise. In my experience, the Advanced exercises are the most difficult. Again, this doesn't mean that if you find an exercise in this category, that you shouldn't use it earlier. Let your instincts be your guide.

Each exercise has the following headings:

Purpose: This says what group members will learn from the exercise and why it is valuable. This section is just for you. You don't need to share it with the members of your group.

Tools: Lists of any tools, i.e. drawing utensils, paper and so on, that you might need to do the exercise.

Notes to the Leader: Notes that would be helpful for a leader to read before working on the exercise.

Procedure: The exercise itself. The exercise can be done as written or adapted and changed to fit your needs.

Feedback Session: Advice and suggestions on how to process each exercise and questions you might want to ask your group.

Many of the exercises include headings entitled:

Movement: The movement part of the exercise.

Group Improvisation: An improvisation involving your entire group.

Two-Person Improvisation: An improvisation involving two people.

Divide Into Pairs: A part of an exercise done in pairs.

Divide into groups of 3 or 4: A part of an exercise is done in small groups.

Variations: Ideas on how you might vary the basic exercise. You can add to it, change it and adapt it to fit your own personal circumstances and purpose.

Symbolic drawing: A part of an exercise, which involves drawing.

Assignments: Things for group members to do on their own that compliment the work done in the group.

NOTE: I have written each exercise the way that I present it to my groups. Please feel free to change the order, if that better suits your needs.

Teach only love, for that is what you are.
— A Course in Miracles

The Art of Group Leadership

Tips for Leading the Exercises

Jumping Into the Water

It's important that you throw your group into the water. When you begin an exercise, you can answer one or two questions from the group and then begin the exercise. Don't give them time to think or analyze. Believe me, they will want to try to figure it out beforehand. You'll see many eyes roll upward as they think about the exercise. They might be thinking of the 'right' way to do the exercise, which is exactly what you don't want them to do. The more they get used to risking and jumping in, the easier their work, and your work will be.

I think of one event that happened as I encouraged my groups to jump into the water. The first time I took my one-year-old daughter, Julie, to a lake, I saw her do something that was amazing. My three-year-old son, Josh, was playing in shallow water. Julie saw him, walked into the lake and just kept on walking. I watched her thinking, "Of course, she'll stop," but she didn't. She kept walking until the water was almost over her head. I grabbed her; she coughed a bit and was fine. I was amazed at her boldness. She had no fear. I love to encourage participants to just 'keep walking and don't think.' It creates excitement and daring within a group.

To go on meeting anyone where he has been is to miss where he is now.
I have to meet people now or I don't meet them anywhere.
If I meet them in memory, I don't meet THEM, and I am not meeting.
Memory is meeting, and memory is not ME, NOW.

— Barry Stevens, psychologist

Never Explain

When you introduce a new exercise to your group, you don't need to give an explanation of why you're doing the exercise. If someone asks, just say, "Trust me. I will tell you the reasons later." The reasons for not saying your purpose in giving an exercise are as follows:

- You take away the spontaneity and freshness of the exercise if you explain it.
- Participants will analyze the exercise instead of jumping in and experiencing it.
- You stop the flow of energy by explaining it. Explaining an exercise can take away the excitement, the energy and the risk factor.
- Trusting, spontaneity and being bold are important parts of this work. By explaining the reasons for the exercise before you do the exercise, you can inhibit your group's creativity.
- When you trust the creative process and your intuitions, the exercises will flow easily and you will be amazed at what you see happening in your group.

The greatest good you can do for another is not just to share your riches, but to reveal to him his own.

— Benjamin Disraeli, statesman and writer

On Giving Directions

Make sure you repeat the directions so your group won't be confused. The reason for repeating your directions is that often people hear what they want to hear instead of what you have said to them.

You don't need to explain the entire exercise. Only give directions for the part of the exercise that you're about to do. Try to make your directions brief and clear.

Good teaching is more a giving of right questions than a giving of right answers.
— Josef Albers, artist and educator

The Socratic Method

The Socratic Method is when you, the group leader, answer a question by asking a question back to the group. Example: A group member asks you, "I don't understand why we did this exercise. Can you explain why we did it?"

Instead of answering his question, you turn the question back to him and say, "That's a good question. Why do you think we did the exercise?"

If the person has no idea, you can pose the same question to the entire group: "Does anyone know why we did that exercise?"

Someone in the group will answer it, or several members might have their own ideas. In this way, they learn from each other instead of always looking to you for answers.

There is one other way I approach it when someone says that he doesn't know the answer to his own question. I ask, "If you *did* know the answer, what would it be?"

He might say, "I don't know" and I repeat again, "If you *did* know the answer, what would it be?"

Ninety-five percent of the time, they answer their own question. In other words, most of the time people know the answers to their own questions. If you give them the chance to answer their own question first, it builds up confidence and teaches them to trust their own perceptions. Sometimes, someone comes up with another reason why we did an exercise. It may be a reason that I never thought of. When you ask the question, "Why did we do that exercise?" you might receive amazing answers and perceptions for both you and your group.

Courage is resistance to fear, master of fear, not absence of fear.
— Mark Twain, author

Belly Button Theory

Many of these exercises are exciting and some might be scary. When someone in my group says, "That was scary," I explain the Transactional Analysis term, *the Belly Button Theory*. This means that they should see an image of a belly button when they feel scared. One half of the belly button says SCARED. The other half says EXCITED. When they are scared, they merely flip the belly button over the other way, and it will say EXCITED. Many things that are scary can also be exciting. By using this technique, fears can be turned into excitement.

If we did all the things we are capable of doing, we would literally astound ourselves.

— Thomas Alva Edison, inventor

Keeping The Body And Voice Relaxed

During movement work, some people may become tense and stiff. They may not be used to moving their bodies in a physical way. It is crucial that you remind them during each exercise to keep their body relaxed. They can send liquid to any part that feels tense. The *Relaxation Series* (p. 71) and *Energizing Series* (p. 75) given at the beginning of each session helps to relax and center their energy and is invaluable for wiping the day's slate clean. Members may come from a stressful day at work. This easy 10-15 minute warm-up starts each class with a calming relaxation series and helps keep their bodies and voices relaxed during the session.

It is helpful for them to just hang over from the waist and relax their whole body while hanging over. Their voices and bodies must be free and loose at all times. Their creative juices will flow easily and their creative impulses will rarely be blocked if they keep their bodies and voices relaxed.

We follow a path through the heart, and into the Presence.
When we get to the Presence through the heart – yum, yum, yum.

— Ram Dass

Do Not Allow Applause

Tell your group that there should not be applause after an improvisational scene. The reasons are as follows:

- Applause sets up competition within your group. If you allow applause, one person might receive more applause than another person. I used to allow applause when I first started teaching, but I saw how destructive it was.
- Members work for applause, which makes them more result-oriented rather than **process**-oriented. People may tend to try to be funny or 'cute.'
- Applause sets up the feeling that a performance has been given. Your participants will try to be 'good' or 'funny.' Applause can create stress because each person wants to be 'the best' and 'succeed.' They want to do the exercise correctly. Allowing applause totally negates the contract, which states NO RIGHT and NO WRONG in this kind of work.
- Your participants will feel wonderful that they did the exercise and risked. They won't be as connected to **how** it looked or how what they did was received. The focus will be on **process** and not a performance.

The shell must break before the bird can fly.
— Lord Alfred Tennyson, English poet

Notes On Setting Up Improvisations

Many of the exercises involve two-, three- and four-person improvisations, and there are many improvisations involving your whole group. Improvisations are fun and they create a wonderful feeling of sharing and unity within your group. Here are a few ideas.

1. You can, in most cases, substitute a man for a woman or a woman for a man. The gender usually doesn't matter.

2. You can use the two-person improvisations as a three-person improvisation and just add one more person. If you are attracted to a three-person improvisation and just want to make it a two-person improvisation, that's fine. Adapt them in any way you see fit.

3. Ask your groups to take risks. They might not know anything about the character or situation they are in. That doesn't matter. They can make it up. Example: I tell a member that they are a famous race car driver, and they know nothing about race cars. Who cares? If they believe what they're saying, we'll believe it. That's the fun of improvisation.

4. The people in the improvisations must always have an objective, action and obstacle. See Appendix J for a Glossary of Terms.

5. Conflict is the essence of all drama and comedy. Build a conflict into your improvisations.

6. You can decide the characters first or the place of the scene first. It doesn't matter. Example: You decide on a flower shop and have two elderly gentlemen walk in.

7. Don't be surprised if members start to invent their own conflicts as their scene progresses. Once they begin to feel comfortable improvising, your group will fly!

8. There will be times when you will ask them to create their own improvisations from scratch. They'll have had plenty of experience doing them already, so they'll be excited to structure their own scenes.

9. Your group will be doing improvisations with two and more people. They will have time to rehearse. It is important that you tell them that when they do it for the group, the improvisation may change, and that's fine. They are rehearsing to understand the tools and techniques you are teaching. They don't have to "hold on" to exactly what they did in the short rehearsals.

10. It's wonderful to place funny scenes in serious places. Example: Two women meet in a funeral home at a wake. They planned a double wedding for their sons, and now one woman wants to change the plans. You can also have a serious scene in a funny place. Example: Two

brothers meet in an amusement park. They lost each other during the war and have not seen each other in thirty years.

11. In many of the exercises you will ask your client/group to create a character. Refer to Appendix E: Autobiographical Questions for Character. You may think of many other questions to ask as they are creating characters. This list can jump-start your imagination.

Imagination grows by exercise.
— Anonymous

End Each Improv On An Up Note

An up note is a place just after a climax, a laugh or a peak moment. Always keep your *audience* wanting **more**. As the improvisation ends, they should feel "Oh, I wish we could have gone on longer!" You give each improvisation a sense of show and theater. Begin each improvisation by saying "Curtain" and end each improvisation by saying "Curtain." This creates the feeling that a curtain is being raised and then lowered at the end of the scene.

Certain improvisations will be of a serious nature. They can be ended on an up note, at some emotional climax in the situation. It is important to never let an improvisation peter out and fade away. They should always end with everyone on pins and needles or at least excited by what they have seen.

In teaching, you cannot see the fruit of a day's work. It is invisible and remains so, maybe for twenty years.
— Jacques Barzun, American historian

Drawing With Your Opposite Hand

When you give symbolic drawing assignments, ask that each person draw with their non-dominant hand. In other words, if you are right-handed, draw with your left hand. If you are left-handed, draw with your right hand. There are several reasons why this is important.

Your non-dominant hand is much freer and more intuitive. It is difficult to control a drawing with your non-dominant hand. The drawings will have a feeling of spontaneity and innocence. The child-like qualities of each drawing will often yield valuable personal insights. Drawing with the non-dominant hand takes away the pressure of making their drawing perfect or even pretty.

People get in touch with their love of drawing and scribbling and they can float away their judgmental voices that say, "You can't draw." I once asked a group I was teaching, "How many of you were told that you couldn't draw well when you were a child?" Ninety-five percent of hands went up. Once you can erase or float those voices and judges away, you'll be amazed at the drawings your group does. They will reach a point where they're excited when they see the drawing paper and crayons in the room.

Imagination is more important than knowledge.

— Albert Einstein, theoretical physicist and philosopher

How To Image

Often, in giving directions to an exercise, you'll say, "Close your eyes and get an image." Some students can image easily; others might have some difficulties. You can tell your group the following: "Imaging can be done with any of the five senses – sight, touch, taste, hearing and smell. It doesn't necessarily mean that you have to see something. The images don't have to be fleshed out. You might feel a feeling in your body, instead of actually seeing an image."

Before doing an image exercise, you ask your group to close their eyes and see their bedroom. Then they open their eyes and describe what they 'saw.' They can also 'taste' their favorite food, feel 'as if' they were touching something really soft, or remembering a time when they felt peaceful. These preliminary exercises all show your group that it's easy and wonderful to image.

To have an image is to have a body change. They might feel a physical kinesthetic change happening inside their bodies. When you say, "Remember a time when you felt really excited," they might feel a kinesthetic response at the same time.

Tell your group that they can use imaging in real-life situations. If they were going for a job interview that might be stressful, they could remember a time that was peaceful in their lives. They'll have a greater appreciation for how useful imaging can be in daily life. Imaging is a wonderful way to center and will be a tool they'll have at their command forever.

Who can afford to live without beauty? Beauty fills us with passion; it graces us with joy and lights up our existence. A landscape, a piece of music, a film, a dance—suddenly all dreariness is gone, we are left bewitched, we are dazzled. If we get lost in dark despair, beauty takes us back to the Center. With its colorful spontaneity, it regenerates our lives. Beauty challenges the force of gravity. It is the promise of a world where all contradictions and pain have vanished. Embrace it, and all greed disappears, for in that moment you are completely disinterested, you are innocent.

— Piero Ferrucci, psychotherapist and philospher

Objectives Of Guided Imagery

There are several objectives in using guided imagery. It's an invaluable tool because it creates another tool for creativity. After participants get an image, they can physically move to that image. They can 'become' the image or a part of the image. They can draw the image. As they move to or draw their images, an unconscious bond is created between themselves and their images. They have experienced a part of themselves in a different way.

Participants can then share their images with each other, through movement, drawing or language. Guided imagery stimulates imaginations and provides a rich way of learning and experiencing the world. It encourages people to trust and act upon their impulses.

Kind words can be short and easy to speak, but their echoes are truly endless.
— Mother Teresa

Creating Safety In Guided Imagery

In the exercises involving guided imagery, say to your group before you begin, "I am just a guide. In the guided imagery, you don't have to follow exactly what I say. I won't be going too fast or too slow. You can go at the pace you need to go. Just use my voice as a guide."

It is important to tell your group that in guided imagery work, THEY ARE IN CHARGE. If something comes up in a visualization that they don't want to deal with, they can let it go or float it away. Let them know that they are in charge of the imaging, not you.

Saying this to your group will create a safety net for them. You never know whether something you might say could trigger a highly emotional memory that they might not want to recall. If they know they can change what they hear, ignore it, or float away any unpleasant image, they will feel empowered. They will feel safer doing guided imagery work.

There is no passion to be found playing small —
in settling for a life that is less than the one you are capable of living.
— Nelson Mandela, South African political leader

Pick A Number

In many of the movement exercises you can decide how much you want your group to exaggerate or blow up the movement. You give them a number from one to ten. The number ten is as large and big a movement as a person can make. The number one is the tiniest movement a person can make. Often, you will give your group the choice of how big or small they would like to make the movement. They can explore going slowly from one to ten with the movements. They see how each number feels in their bodies.

Experience is not what happens to you; it is what you do with what happens to you.
— Aldous Huxley, British author

Verbal And Physical Grounding After An Exercise Is Completed

What is grounding? Grounding gives your group a sense of completion. Often participants are so involved in the exercise that it's challenging to come back together as a group and process the work that was done. Several of the exercises are intense and people can feel spacey and not quite 'here' after the exercise ends. Grounding brings each person back to the present. Grounding an exercise prepares them to do another exercise or go to their next activity.

Verbal grounding is a time for sharing, discussion and processing an exercise. It is crucial to ground each exercise because each person will have feelings, insights and even breakthroughs that they might wish to share with the group.

You can also divide your group into pairs, so each person grounds his/her insights and learnings with a partner. Have each person find someone they don't know well. At one point in their sharing, you can say, "Freeze. You have two minutes left. Are you saying what you would like to say? Is there anything else you would like to share?" This can create a more intense sharing and less holding back. Always give a one-minute warning so know that soon the sharing will be over. It is important to say, "You can share as little or as much as you like. Do what feels comfortable for you." The sharings are usually five to ten minutes per person.

I love to physically ground the group after an intense exercise. Physical grounding is when you do movement work after an exercise ends. When people ground in their bodies, it helps to bring them back to the present.

Making physical contact with others in a silly way is fun and helps bring everyone back to reality. It helps to break the intensity after a serious exercise. You're changing the energy in the room. Here are a few you can do:

1. Have everyone in your group bend their knees. Each person walks around with bent knees and meets other group members. When two people meet, they clap each other's hands and say, "Wow, wow, wow." Then each person moves on and finds a new partner. They repeat this several times. It is a silly exercise and it breaks the tension and brings each person back to the present moment.

2. Your group makes a large circle and does a square dance move called a Dosey-do. People lock arms with the person on their right and continue around the circle locking arms with the next person. They are vocalizing whatever they choose to say. This is also silly and changes the energy in the room by bringing everyone back to the present moment.

3. Jumping jacks also change the energy in the group. Everyone stands with their feet together and arms by their side. Then each person jumps and widens their feet and lifts their arms over their heads. They yell "WAYHOO!" as they do ten jumping jacks.

Basically any physical movement, which the group can do together and is simple and fun, is a way of grounding your group.

Journal writing is another way to ground. You can give your group five or ten minutes to write any reflections or ideas they discovered. If they want more time for writing, you merely say, "Take some time later today or tomorrow to write other ideas or insights you had while doing the exercise."

After you've done several different grounding exercises, a group can come together and sit in a large circle. You can ask, "Would anyone like to share anything about what happened to you during the exercise?" It can be powerful for one participant to share his experience in front of the whole group. We experience something differently when we ground it through movement, writing, sharing in pairs and then in sharing our experience before a group. There is usually only time for a few people to share in front of the group.

It gives a sense of accomplishment because they can verbalize what each exercise meant to them. In this grounding session, you can also give the reasons why an exercise was done. It is often best to first ask them why **they** think you gave the exercise. This encourages your group to look to each other for answers instead of to you. You always want to do things that **empower** your participants and the group as a whole.

Painting is just another way of keeping a diary.
— Pablo Picasso, artist

Tools And Clothing

In order to do the exercises involving symbolic drawing, you provide the following materials:

- Crayons and markers in the middle of the circle. They pick what colors they want to use.
- A pad of 18" x 24" newsprint
- Drawing boards to put underneath the newsprint

Participants bring their own journals and pen. Loose-fitting clothing should be worn for flexibility of movement. They should wear clothing that they don't mind getting dirty, since the floor is used for some of the work. Soft-soled shoes are recommended. High heels and fancy clothing aren't appropriate for a group meeting.

When you get right down to the root of the meaning of the word "succeed,"
you find it simply means to follow through.

— F. W. Nichol, business executive

Tips for Leading Your Group

The First Meeting

The first group meeting is important because it sets the tone for the group experience. I do a number of things that can help create a safe and trusting environment. You would adapt 1a) and b) if your group meets one time only.

1. State the Ground Rules or Group Contract:

   a) Members MUST be on time to each meeting. If they're late one time without a very good excuse, they are given a warning. If they're late twice, they are asked to leave the group. It is crucial that you enforce this rule. People will tend to take you and themselves seriously if they know you mean business. It can ruin the trust, safety and cohesiveness of a group if someone comes in late. When participants are on time, it creates respect and a sense of professionalism with the work.

   b) A meeting is never missed, except for an emergency. To build group cohesion, everyone must be at each meeting so they can participate and support each other's work. The group support for each person is crucial. When one person has a breakthrough, the group as a whole goes through the roof, so to speak. It's an exciting moment.

   c) There is no right or wrong in this work. Most educational systems stress a correct way, or a right way, and an incorrect way, or a wrong way, for things to be done. In these exercises, they will think to themselves, "This is right," or "I did that exercise incorrectly." Thinking this way will freeze their creative juices. The theory of no right or wrong takes away all of the judgments people make about themselves. THERE ARE NO JUDGMENTS. Say to your members, "The group is not judging you. I am not judging you. And most important, please don't judge yourself. Judgment kills creativity. The atmosphere we want to create together is one that is respectful, positive, open and non-judgmental. When your inner judge appears, put him on a piece of chiffon and float him away. It is important that we are all free to take risks, be silly and PLAY." There is an exercise called *Float Your Judges Away* (p. 109), which helps in this process.

d) Confidentiality is crucial. I say, "Nothing shared within the group goes any further than this group. You may tell your friends and colleagues about the exercises we did, but please don't share what people say during an exercise." You want them to feel free to share who they are, and confidentiality is key for this to happen. I state this and then ask everyone to raise their hands if they agree to this part of the contract. Doing this physical action grounds their commitment to confidentiality.

e) Send positive energy to each person working. This positive energy is an important part of the contract. When people feel loved, supported, accepted and cared for, they grow.

f) Respect is crucial. It may seem silly to state this, but it's important. There's no violence or disrespect to anyone in the class. We don't touch each other unless we have permission to do so.

2. Tell the group something about yourself, your background and your working philosophy so they know something about you.

3. If appropriate, let students in long-term groups know how and when you can be reached for questions or consultations.

4. Have members introduce themselves, telling something about who they are, what they hope to get out of the group, why they are there, and anything else they would like to share about themselves. This breaks the ice and helps people begin to feel comfortable with each other.

5. Lead the *My Name Is* exercise (p. 67). This exercise is one of my favorites because it opens people up and lets each person risk and jump in the water.

One of the glories of working in the theater or in films is the teamwork, the trust,
the cool trust needed to overcome the otherwise superhuman task of realizing the imagination.
— Laurence Olivier, actor

Atmosphere Of A Group

The key to leading your group successfully is your enthusiasm and protective, nurturing care. You must love the people you are working with, respect each person's dignity and appreciate their vulnerability. Whenever a person is exposed before a group, whether participating in an exercise or doing an exercise alone, that person is emotionally naked and therefore must be protected.

You set the tone for the group. If the environment is warm, caring and loving, people will feel safe and be able to take risks. An accepting group encourages experimentation and thereby, growth. A judgmental group makes people nervous, uptight and afraid.

Your aim is to stimulate and ignite interest by your enthusiasm. This approach fosters growth and challenges each person to be his most creative self. The environment is filled with positive energy. Expect the best from your group and you'll never be disappointed. In a class I attended, the teacher told a story of a study that was conducted on teachers' expectations. One group of teachers was given ten students and were told that they were exceptional students. In fact, the students were not exceptional. But the teachers treated them as if they were exceptional students and their work was indeed, exceptional. People usually live up to your expectations. If you radiate the feeling, "Of course you can do this work. You are gifted." members will take off and even exceed your expectations.

Many years ago, I took a Prosperity Workshop for Entrepreneurs. There were fifteen people in our group. Once our leader asked us to bring in materials to build something at our next class meeting. There were several engineers in the class whom I knew would build amazing structures. All I could think to bring in were some index cards, scissors and scotch tape. At the next class, our leader said to us, "Build something." Those were the only instructions.

I thought of making a bridge with my index cards from one chair to the table where we sat. I made the thin bridge about ½" wide. It was suspended between one chair and the wooden table. I thought it looked pretty cool.

Of course, the engineers' structures were incredibly complicated and beautiful. It was time to process the exercise. Our leader glanced over at my thin bridge and smirked. "Whose is this?" she asked.

"That's mine," I said brightly. We still had no idea why we built these structures.

She said, "This is a model for how you do your business. How do your students find you? There is no way to get to your bridge!"

Without missing a beat, but still being respectful, I spontaneously said, "My students are angels. They fly to get there." She looked at me and said nothing.

I did think about this experience afterwards and thought that what I said was true. My students are angels and they can do anything. That's truly how I perceive the people I teach. When I went into teaching thirty years ago, I didn't believe that, but after several years of teaching, I knew people could do anything and it's glorious to teach them knowing and believing this fact.

When I taught over 120 physician workshops around the United States, the physicians role-played their most challenging patients. I wanted them to understand what the patient was feeling, so I had the doctor play the patient as well as play the doctor. I had 'alter egos' on each side playing doctor and patient. The 'alter ego' would say what the doctor or patient was feeling.

There were between twelve and forty physicians in a workshop. One woman had permission to observe one of my workshops. She came up to me afterwards and said, "It was amazing how you got all of the doctors to participate. Do you know how you did that?" I hadn't really thought about it. She continued. "You just *expected* that they would want to go up front and role-play, and you made it fun." A leader's expectations of what their group can do are key to leading a successful group. When you know they can do anything you ask, they will.

Psychology Of Group Dynamics

Psychology and knowledge of group dynamics is essential for group leaders. There are several things that you can do to make your group cohesive:

- Listen to what they say. Use the Listening Exercise. It's an invaluable tool for creating trust, mutual respect and encouraging students to open up to each other.

- Know how to read non-verbal body language and behavior. Often people say one thing, but mean something else. When you're attuned to listening to their body and gestures as well as their voices, you'll understand them better and what they are trying to say. Knowing how to read a person's subtext, or what a person is saying between the words they are speaking, is crucial.

- Care about each member of your group. Let them know that you care about them. Remember you are only teaching love.

- Trust your intuitions. Listen to your inner voices. Often you may hear a voice telling you something that you think is ridiculous. Listen to it. Trust your instincts and follow those voices. They come from your most creative self.

- Risk. You as a leader will risk and it's important that you stress risking to your group. Risk is when we go into a new territory that might be scary, exciting, exhilarating and fun. When they see you trying new ideas and risking, they will feel encouraged and supported to 'jump off more cliffs.' The unknown can be stimulating and keeps you and your group on its toes. When you risk, you are trusting your intuition and telling your judges to go away. Your judges are those negative inner voices who try to stop you from taking risks. Judges come in the form of your parents, teachers, and the parts of you that are scared to let go and fly.

- Teach discipline. Discipline creates freedom. A ballet dancer can't do a leap and fly unless she has a very strong plié, which is bending her knees before she takes off. When a dancer bends her knees before leaping in the air, she goes much higher. She has grounded herself in her plié and can then fly! When your group sees how committed and disciplined you are, they will follow your lead and take the work as seriously, and playfully, as you do.

- Be patient. Trust yourself and trust each person's own process. Tell your group, "I believe that each person is exactly where they need to be right now." It is important to be patient because students grow and risk at their own pace. All they need is your guidance, support and love and they will thrive. I remember one acting student who was never quite relaxed on stage. In our last class, she did her final acting scene and she was fantastic. She was real, in the moment and had integrated the various techniques she had learned throughout the year. I asked her how she thought she did in her scene. She said, "Great!" I asked her, "Why was it so great this time?" She replied, "Because I didn't care at all what you thought!" I always told my students "Do this for you, not for me." Previous to that day, she had seen me as her judge and that inhibited her work. At last, she let her judge go, and her work soared. She finally got it. I had to trust her process and knew she would eventually get there. No teacher ever knows what a student has been though in her life. We have to trust that with enough patience and love, the person will get from our workshops what they most need.

- And lastly, "To thine own self be true." Examine your values and beliefs. Always make sure you are honest with yourself and your group. They, in turn, will be honest with you and with each other.

The great teacher is not the man who supplies the most facts,
but the one in whose presence we become different people.
— Ralph Waldo Emerson, poet and essayist

Be Adaptable

Even if you master every skill of group leadership, you will not always be in control of what happens in your groups, so you must be adaptable. Be prepared to engage with the unexpected.

In my first year of teaching acting, when I was twenty-five years old, I gave the group the Object Exercise. I ask students to find an object in the room and hold it in their hand. I tell them, "This object means more to you than anything in the world. This is your most favorite object." I ask the group to make a large circle and sit down. Two people go into the center of the circle. One may be asked to bring his object; one may be asked not to bring his object. With one pair of students, I asked one man to bring his object into the circle and one woman to not bring her object into the circle. It's a non-verbal exercise. The young man misunderstood the directions and when it was his turn, he took off all of his clothes! I sat there, along with the other forty people in the group. I presented a calm exterior, but inside I was thinking, "If my boss walks by the room, I am finished." The room had glass windows! After he put his clothes back on, we discussed what had happened in a way that left him feeling supported and cared for by the group. We understood why he did what he did, and I took responsibility for not having explained the exercise clearly.

It's important to stay open to what is happening each moment. You might have an exercise that doesn't feel right to do at the time. Go with that intuition. Use another exercise or adapt the one you have already planned. Not every exercise you use will be perfect; adjust it if you need to. Change it on the spot. When I give my weekend retreats, I have an outline of an exercise. But the exercise creates itself as we go along. It is very thrilling to work in this way.

Spontaneity is important. If you are sensitive to the mood of the group and your mood, you'll feel free to experiment and try new things. Be aware of your group's rhythms. The *process* is the key, not the result.

One last point on being adaptable. I create a time in the class when people can ask questions. This usually happens at the beginning of a day-long workshop or right after our *Relaxation Series* (p. 71) and *Energizing Series* (p. 75). In one class, a student asked, "How do you play innocence?" How do we get in touch with that part of ourselves?" I heard the question at the beginning of one workshop and my mind started racing. Later in the day, we did an hour-long exercise on this question. At a retreat three months later, I structured a five-hour improvisation on her question. By being open to the moment, I was able to develop a whole new exercise.

When you're adaptable, you focus on the process. If you trust the moment, you're always in process. It's an exciting way to work with a group. It may seem risky, but it has never failed me.

The most effective way to achieve right relations with any living thing is to look for the best in it,
and then help that best into the fullest expression.

— J. Allen Boone, writer

Conflicts And Control

Be aware that someone may, unknowingly or knowingly, try to manipulate the group. Example: One person is always late and wants you to take on the role of his parent or boss and tell him, week after week, that he is thoughtless for being late. Try to break that pattern. You can say, "If you are late again, as I stated in the Contract in the first meeting, you will be asked to leave the group." The rest of your group will respect you for sticking to the stated contract and then following through on it.

If someone verbally attacks you, realize that YOU are not the target. People often use transference and projection at times when they're under stress. In other words, any figure in authority can remind a participant of a parent, teacher, or boss. If someone becomes angry, don't get angry with him. Stay calm. Listen, repeat what he says and give yourself time to think about how you would like to respond. Always deal with that person in a caring supportive way. Remember, you're a role model. You might want to role-reverse and feel like you were the person who became angry. **Anger is usually a cry for help.**

Once you stand in their shoes, it's easier to see where their anger is coming from. You can also 'fair witness' or stand outside of the situation and observe it. This gives you a certain amount of objectivity and distance. This technique lets you see the situation in an objective way.

Deal with conflicts as they come up. Don't sweep them under the rug. Go over the situation with your group if the situation is presenting problems. Listen to what is said. When I first started teaching, a student verbally attacked me. She had been difficult to work with and in frustration, I snapped at her. Later, I apologized to her in front of the entire group. The person, as it turned out, never did quite accept my apology, but I felt good about how I had handled the situation. Group leaders certainly aren't perfect and we are always learning.

Realize that in a conflict situation that you can't control everything. You can't win everyone over 100% of the time. Realize you're human, not super-human. Sometimes group leaders forget their own vulnerabilities and humanness.

An incredible incident happened when I was brought in to teach a three-hour workshop on Improvisation to high school principals. I spoke for twenty minutes about my philosophy of teaching improvisation and then said, "Okay, let's move the chairs away and do some improvisation." At that point about sixty percent of the group LEFT! I was surprised. You can't TALK about improvisation, you have to DO it.

They were unwilling to risk their 'image' and plunge in. After the workshop ended, the man who hired me came up to me and said, "Oh, this is common. Most of them don't want anything experiential." I wish he had told me that beforehand. The forty percent who stayed were appreciative and hopefully learned a lot about improvisation and how valuable it can be for their teachers to use in the classroom.

The best teachers teach from the heart, not from the book.
— Anonymous

Have High Expectations

In my physician workshops, many doctors don't know that we will be doing psychodrama and role-playing. When I ask the question, "Who here hates role-playing?" several hands will go up. And after the workshop, many say, "I am now a role-playing junkie."

The doctors play their patients so they can stand in their patient's shoes and feel how their patients feel. I have the expectation that they will *love* role-playing and become totally involved in the many scenarios we enact. Some physicians have even broken down crying when they stood in their patient's shoes and received bad news like, "Your cancer has come back." They learned from each other how to handle difficult situations and it is wonderful for me to see them interact in heartfelt and vulnerable ways.

The bottom line is, I love surprising people with what will happen in a workshop. When you surprise people, they don't have a chance to think, and they often do the exercises with great abandon. Your positive energy and excitement rubs off on your participants. They trust you and know that you are coming from your heart in your teaching.

It's only when we're willing to be vulnerable, unprotected by fixed ideas, traditions and habitual ways, that the adventure of self-discovery, the inward voyage can begin.
— Vimala Thakar, Indian social activist and spiritual teacher

Vulnerability

When you, as the group leader, are vulnerable, you're saying to each member, "If you choose, you are free to be vulnerable, too." By vulnerability, I mean sharing events that have happened in your life to show your humanness. You can relate personal experiences, when appropriate, that show your vulnerability. I remember when I was coaching a scene that had to do with a dysfunctional family.

I asked the students doing the scene to attend an Adult Children of Alcoholics meeting and do some observations. In that sharing, I told them that I had been to several meetings and they helped in my own healing. I didn't go into detail, but it's important to show your vulnerability and let your students know that you're a human being, too. In other words, don't hide behind your role.

Over the piano was printed a notice:
Please do not shoot the pianist. He is doing his best.
— Oscar Wilde, Irish dramatist, poet and wit

Suspend Judgments

Suspend judgments of what you think a person in your group is capable of accomplishing. Always say something affirmative about their work and they will astound you. Nothing succeeds like success. Example: One man walked into my class. He was forty-years-old and looked like a walking board. He showed no feeling and spoke in a monotone. I thought to myself, "What on earth is he doing here?" But I gave him support and encouragement. We had a *Perfect People Party* (p. 111) where each person comes as a Perfect Person — a Perfect Banker, Perfect Go-Go Dancer, and so on. Each person in the class comes as a character and stays in character for three hours. He came to the party as a Perfect Sleaze. This was out of character for him. He grew in leaps and bounds. He was more relaxed and vulnerable. He connected on a whole different level to people in the group improvisations. If you have no preconceived notions about what people can do, you will always be surprised. Your participants are opening up their channels of creativity and you never know when those juices will begin to flow.

We can do no great things, only small things with great love.
— Mother Teresa

Constructive Feedback

How do you give constructive feedback? Here are some tips:

- Be gentle and caring.

- Be specific.

- Always start with positive feedback. People listen to you if they know what worked well. If you start with critical comments, their ears may close and they won't hear anything that you're saying after your critical remarks.

- Praise experimentation and risk-taking.

- Ask each person the process they went through. This clarifies their own process and gives you clues on what they did and how they approached each exercise.

- Support all efforts made, however small.

- Give feedback with kindness and care in areas that need work.

- Always stress, as you did in the first meeting, that there is no right and no wrong in this work. There are only *different ways of doing things.* This relieves a lot of tension during the feedback session.

A person travels to discover himself.
— James Russell Lowell, poet, editor and diplomat

Healing

To say that this creative work heals people is an understatement. I know that the people I've taught have truly been my healing. It is impossible to tell you how many students have told me during a class or after the class had ended, how much the class meant to them. The most common comment has been, "This class has changed my life. I learned so much about myself in the most incredible ways." And I, as the group leader did not change them. The group and what happened in the class facilitated their growth, creativity, and joy.

One major factor is creating change in people is laughter. If your group can laugh a lot, that's wonderful. Warmth, vulnerability and humor go hand in hand.

- The Exercises are the foundation.

- The Contract is the discipline (see p. 35).

- The group atmosphere of acceptance and love is the healing. For many people, my group was the first class experience where they felt safe, accepted and loved. Love heals. And that's all we are learning and teaching — to be love, and send love in all that we do.

I have come here, not to teach you, but to love you.
Love itself will teach you.
— Yogi Amrit Desai, spiritual teacher

Love Defined

The center, core and essence of this book is **love**. If love is left out of group leadership, the work will be empty and soulless. You can still use these techniques, but they will lack passion and heart. This book will only serve as a manual instead of a guide. Love must be woven into each exercise and interaction. Love is open-ended. It's a process. Someone in a workshop I once attended asked the question, "What is love?"

Another person responded by saying, "There are three kinds of love. I love you. I am in love with you. I am loving you."

I prefer the third one. "I am loving you," is ongoing, active and you can always start anew.

The easiest way to talk about what I mean when I say "Love your students", is to tell you about three experiences I had with three different group leaders. Two of the three leaders loved the people they were leading. First and foremost, these teachers were genuinely interested in each person in the group.

Bernie Siegel, a surgeon, led Exceptional Cancer Patient groups in New Haven, Connecticut, and has written many books. He taught a two-day workshop called The Psychology of Illness and The Art of Healing. There were one hundred and eighty people in the workshop. It was an incredible group experience. Why? I felt bathed in his warmth, love and care as I sat there. That may sound a bit corny, but he really 'touched' each person with his total acceptance and love.

Not only was he vulnerable as he led the group, but by just being himself, everyone in the group opened up. I remember he told a story of a woman who came to see him. She was a wreck. She smelled and was dirty. He didn't treat her with any medications, but merely talked to her and she talked to him.

He listened. Within several months, she cleaned herself up. He saw the *best* in her. What did Bernie do? As he said, "I just accepted her as she was." Bernie's motto for his work and organization is "LOVE HEALS" and he practices it.

Marsha Sinetar is the author of *Ordinary People as Monks and Mystics*. She is another incredible leader. She had the same qualities as Bernie. She led a day-long workshop with sixty people. One of her gifts was that she validated each person's comments and made sure that each person felt valued and **needed** as part of the group. She would restate a person's comments and each person felt heard and **important**.

Another gift, besides the wonderful way she responded to each person, was that she cared about the people she was teaching. She shared parts of herself in an honest and sincere way. She wanted to get to know us. Marsha and Bernie never set themselves up on a pedestal. They related from their heart to each one of us. They had a desire to touch us with their words and spirit. They were concerned about what they were teaching; yet the people in the group came first. Or maybe a better way of saying it is, that their caring went hand in hand with what they were teaching. Their caring **was** their teaching!

They saw the **best** in us and in the potentiality of each person as well as the group. With the feeling of total acceptance and love from them, we wanted to share who we were, not just with Bernie and Marsha, but also with each other. The group, as a whole, felt nurtured, protected and valued.

On the other side of the scale, I took a one-day workshop with a famous teacher, whose name I won't mention. I came home after the workshop feeling empty, frustrated and edgy. Why? She set herself apart from us. She was an island. There was no bridge between her and her students. Her subject was important. Her students were not. She was knowledgeable on her subject, but I kept thinking as I listened to her, "What's missing?"

At the lunch break, I asked a friend of mine, "Who *is* she?" I felt I couldn't touch her. She certainly didn't want to touch us. I didn't know who she was. Her ego got in the way of her being open and vulnerable. She wasn't unkind. She was formal and distant. And I knew, at the same time, she was scared to be vulnerable and close to us. The best word to describe her was to say she was masked. The students seldom asked questions and people seemed stiff and somewhat guarded.

Later that evening, I thought to myself, "It's not what you teach but **how** you teach it." I learned the material she taught me, but I felt empty. Her teaching could have been so much more powerful if she had shown us that she genuinely cared about us. How, you might ask, could she have done that? When someone contributed to the group or made a comment she said "Yes," and went right on with her own thought, as if she didn't hear the person. Perhaps it would have helped if she had paused when she heard a question or comment. She might have responded in a personal way to the questions asked and the contributions made in the workshop.

The mediocre teacher tells. The good teacher explains.
The superior teacher demonstrates. The great teacher inspires.
— William Arthur Ward, author

Question Sheet

Whether you're teaching a day-long workshop or a longer class, it's valuable to have what I call a Question Sheet. The group asks any questions they have. You can answer them after lunch or at some point during the day. During a ten-week workshop, I may answer the questions during the fifth or sixth meeting.

Each person comes to a workshop for a different reason. Many have questions they want answered and it's wonderful to have them voice their questions. One person's question is usually of interest to other members of the group. Seeing their questions and concerns helps you structure the exercises and address their questions throughout the day or throughout the duration of your time together.

You might even change an exercise or add something to your agenda that you hadn't planned. What a great way to trust the moment.

There are no problems, only opportunities to be creative.
— Dorye Roettger, author

Tips for Handling Problems

This section will give you some ideas on how to handle problems within your group. The key to handling problems is that you trust the moment. You're asking your members to do the same as they explore their own unique creativity. Therefore, when a problem arises, trust that you will do what needs to be done and handle the situation in a loving and caring way.

This section includes the most common problem areas I've had in leading groups. I'll tell you what the problem was, how it was handled and what seemed to work the best. I'll also tell you what problems had no solutions and how I dealt with *that* as a problem and challenge. The problem areas fall into ten categories:

1. Someone who has problems with the exercise
   What do you do if someone misinterprets or misunderstands an exercise?
   What do you do if there is little participation or enthusiasm for the exercise?
   What do you do if the exercise bombs and doesn't work?

2. A member who has difficulty with another member or members in the group

3. A member who has personal problems that affect the group

4. A member who has difficulty with the leader

5. Setting boundaries between the leader and the group

6. Setting boundaries between group members

7. Someone who has difficulty with the contract

8. The atmosphere in the room is tense

9. Miscellaneous problems

10. Problems that have no solutions

1. Someone who has problems with the exercise

What do you do if someone misinterprets or misunderstands the exercise? You can say, "Perhaps I didn't explain it clearly. Let me explain it again." Always see the misunderstanding as being *your* problem, not the group's problem. You didn't give the directions clearly enough. Maybe the person wasn't listening or paying attention, but if *one* person misunderstood the directions, then probably other members misunderstood the directions as well.

If someone misinterprets the exercise after it has been completed, you might say, "I hadn't thought of the exercise in this way. What you did was very interesting. What you did was good. There are no mistakes. You heard what you needed to hear and that's fine." ALWAYS be supportive of each member. Never put blame on anyone in your group. This will help to bond the group and creates trust between members and between you and the group. Again, you as the leader may not have explained the exercise clearly enough. NO ONE is wrong in this situation. Your job is to support everyone's growth, even if they misunderstand an exercise.

What do you do if there is little participation or enthusiasm for the exercise? The truth of the matter is that some people are afraid. They've never been in a group that has made demands on them or a group that has asked them to be vulnerable. Your job is to gently push them and encourage them. An example would be if you are doing improvisation and instead of asking for volunteers, you just go up to a person and say, "Oh, you would be perfect for this improvisation." Allow the improvisation to last a minute or so and then give them a lot of encouragement and positive reinforcement when they are done. Nothing succeeds like success. If a member doesn't want to participate, don't force him.

Sometimes, people don't participate because they feel that you or other members of the group are judging them. *Stress again that there is no right or wrong way to do an exercise.* I can't tell you how many hundreds of times I have said that sentence to my groups. Often, I say it as I am giving a new exercise to my group.

Members can be critical and judgmental, not of each other, but of themselves. You can never say the following sentences often enough: "*Remember, there is no right or wrong in this exercise. Whatever you do is fine.*"

If members aren't participating, you can ask them for some solutions. This empowers them to be a part of the problem-solving process. They take ownership of the problem and solutions. I remember one class I taught at a women's college where a problem arose. No one in the group was willing to risk. The students rarely asked questions and the class felt stagnant. I realized this after the third meeting, but kept thinking that things might change. At first, I wanted to give them the benefit of the doubt and attributed their being reserved to being shy.

However, as I became more frustrated, I voiced my thoughts to the group. I said, "I will not spoon feed you. You all must put energy and enthusiasm into this class. It is YOUR class. I can only give you the tools and passion that I have for this work. You have to meet me half-way in this process." I can't remember all that I said, but I was upset and let them know how much I wanted the class to work and how much I cared.

I doubt if any other teacher had spoken to them in this way. I wasn't sure what the outcome would be, but I had to speak my truth. The class changed radically after our discussion. They all participated and were eager and excited to try the exercises. It just took a bit of honesty and risking on my part. The group decided to help me 'carry the ball'. If I hadn't addressed it, it would be like having an elephant in the room. Everyone senses something is wrong, yet no one says anything.

What do you do if the exercise bombs and doesn't work? You can end the exercise, if it hasn't already ended. You can talk about what happened and why the exercise didn't work. In other words, process the experience *briefly* with your group. Don't spend too much time going over why it didn't work, but say what you saw and let them give their feedback. Or you can jump right into another exercise when you see the first exercise isn't working well. Instead of ending the first exercise, you dovetail right into another exercise. You can use the first part of the exercise that didn't work, as a warm up for the second exercise. It's almost like getting right back on a horse that threw you off. You continue the process, but in a different way.

Example: I might start a movement exercise and notice after two minutes that people aren't warmed up. So I will finish the movement part and turn it into a fast physical warm-up so they are prepared to continue with the original exercise. I have often changed the entire exercise on the spot and used another exercise in its place. Sometimes I make up a totally different exercise based on the cues I see happening within the group. It's fun to work this way.

2. A member who has difficulty with another member or members in the group

There are several reasons why this may happen. One person in the group may remind another person of someone they don't like. This is beyond your control. What IS in your control is how you react and handle the situation. And it must be handled. One person sending out bad energy or feelings towards another person can affect the group dynamics. You can handle this situation in several ways.

a) Remind your group, as a whole, how important it is to send positive energy to everyone else in the group. One person may not care for another, but that person hopefully wants the group to work as a whole.

b) If it is getting out of hand, you can meet the two participants privately and try to find out what the problem is. Tell them how their behavior is affecting the group and see if you can work out a solution together. Remember, there is no blame here. You are facilitating a solution that works for everyone.

c) You can place these two members in a fun and crazy improvisation together and see if the process of play can resolve their personality conflicts. Sometimes, they will see each other in a different light in the context of play.

d) If one member is critical in a non-supportive way of another member, you can either interrupt and say, "I understand what you are saying. Can you say it in a supportive way so the person is able to hear you?" One way to help members give constructive feedback to each other is to teach them how to do it. You, as the group leader, are the best example.

e) One last point. Anyone who destructively criticizes another member needs help. The best way to do this is to use an image I call the Snoopy Lick Theory. Example: You are yelling at your dog and he comes up and gives you a big wet lick. Your heart melts. All you have to do is transfer that image to your group member. Try to be loving and gentle with that person. There are times when you may, indeed, not feel gentle inside, but when you act in a gentle way, you DO begin to feel that gentleness inside.

f) It is a good idea to state the terms of the Contract if these kinds of situations begin to come up for you and your group. You can easily set boundaries and remind your group how to give constructive feedback.

3. A member who has personal problems that affect the group

Sometimes you might have a hostile member in your group. Remember that you are not the target of her hostility. She is dealing with personal problems, which are beyond your control. If you find her hostility uncontrollable, you can ask her to leave the group. I would first talk to her in private and see if you can handle it together. I remember one student was upset and I knew that it didn't have anything to do with the group or with the exercise we were doing. I began to feel scared for her. I saw her after our second meeting and recommended that she drop from the group. She agreed and felt relieved to be 'let off the hook' from her commitment to the group and me.

4. A member who has difficulty with the leader

If a member attacks you verbally, take a deep breath to center yourself. Then you can repeat the essence of what the person said so he feels heard. NEVER embarrass a member for his comments to you or his comments to someone else. The Snoopy Lick Theory helps you send love his way. You will be amazed at how quickly the situation is transformed.

Example: A participant might say, "I don't like how you're running this group." You can repeat what he said and ask him how he would like to see the group run. You can say, "I like your suggestions and will consider some of them." Obviously this person is having some difficulties and this is an opportunity for you to give him a chance to vent his frustrations and anxieties. Other members might be feeling the same way, but are afraid to bring it up or to question your authority. You have a lot of power as a group leader. Use it lovingly and wisely.

Sometimes, a group member can be defensive with the leader. The best solution is to be caring and understanding. I remember in one class, I was giving feedback to the student after he had completed the *Song and Dance* exercise (p. 195).

During the feedback session, he glared at me and I thought, "What is he thinking? He looks so angry." I wasn't saying hurtful things to him. I felt I was being kind, supportive and honest in what I saw. At the end of the feedback session I asked him, "Does any of what I said ring true for you?" He slowly said, "Yes." And that was the end of the feedback he gave me. He wasn't ready to tell me his true feelings. I approached him after class and said, "Are you all right?" He melted and said, "How did you know all that stuff about me?" He had tears in his eyes and was incredibly appreciative of the fact that I seemed to know him in a way that most people didn't. The point is, if I had misinterpreted his defensiveness as a negative, I would have been upset. Instead, I saw that he wasn't defensive towards me, but he didn't trust people easily. Therefore, I left the door open to approach him after class. As the weeks progressed, he turned out to be one of the most open and trusting students in the group.

Here is one last story. As one student did her improvisation, I asked her, "What is your objective?" She snapped at me and said, "I don't need anything from anyone. I live alone and I can do everything for myself." I told her that what she was saying might be true, but that in an improvisation, you must have an objective, something you need from the other person. She was angry and had built a wall around herself. At the next class, an amazing thing happened. She volunteered to go first when I asked someone to do the *Song and Dance Exercise*. In this exercise, someone sings a song, any song at all, and I ask them to do it many different ways, i.e. as a tree, as a waitress, as the sky, as a policeman, etc. As she got out of her seat, I had chills. Something special was about the happen. The whole group felt it.

She was an Afro-American woman in her fifties. She stood quietly in front of the group and sang, *We Shall Overcome*. You could hear a pin drop in the room. She was magnificent, vulnerable and in the moment. Her defenses from the last class were gone. The point is, I trusted HER process. She did what she needed to do. She had heard what I said in the previous class, but she needed time to absorb it. Her hostility and frustration had been transformed in a week. She showed passion, trust and vulnerability in sharing her gifts. When I started to give weekend retreats, she attended many of them and was a joy to have in every workshop she attended.

5. Setting boundaries between the leader and the group

It's crucial that you say at your first meeting, "This is NOT a therapy group." (The only time you wouldn't say this is if you were a therapist and running a therapy group.) It's important to tell your group what the focus of the group is. People participate in different groups for different reasons. You MUST set clear guidelines on the kind of material you will be dealing with. I say, "We will be telling each other about ourselves. We will be getting to know each other. But this is NOT a therapy group and we won't get into your 'stuff' in a personal way." It is important to set boundaries within the group.

If issues arise in your group, which could be turned into a therapy session, I recommend that you steer away from it tactfully and with sensitivity. Example: During one exercise, each student was talking about an emotion recall. Each person took a turn for a minute and shared a memory of a beautiful experience she'd had. When one student spoke, she started to cry. She remembered a time ten years ago when she was released from a mental institution and how happy she was. I had no idea she had ever been in a mental institution. She shared her recall. The next person told his story and we continued around the circle as we had planned. Each person took a turn. At the end of the exercise, I asked for feedback and comments. I remember saying to the woman who told her story about the mental institution, "The way you told your story touched me. How do you feel?" She responded, "Oh, I feel wonderful." I didn't probe or ask her personal questions about her situation ten years ago. It wasn't my business. And then the group went on with the day's work.

As the leader, you are always free to ask thought provoking questions, if it's appropriate. Or you may realize that you could be treading on dangerous territory if you ask questions that are too personal and invasive. Being vulnerable is one of the objectives for the exercises in this book. But there's a line between someone being vulnerable by their own choice and your probing too deeply into their personal lives.

If you have a problem with a person going on and on in an inappropriate way about his personal life, you can interrupt and steer the discussion back to the exercise at hand. The group must feel that you're in control and can handle uncomfortable situations if they arise. You, as the group leader, are 'holding' the group as a whole and one of your jobs is to keep everyone safe.

6. Setting boundaries between group members

The personal connections that members have outside of the group time are not within your control. You can focus on trust, confidentiality and respect for each person in the group. When you state the Contract at the first meeting, there is a sense of professionalism expected in the group. I feel this sense of professionalism is usually carried out even with issues that happen outside of the class.

7. Someone who has difficulty with the Contract

If a person is late to a group more than one time, or doesn't do the work assigned, then you must give serious consideration to ask him to leave the group. If any part of the Contract is broken, you must stick to your word as you stated in the first group meeting. Your members will only take the group as seriously as you do.

8. The atmosphere in the room is tense

Another incident happened that could have turned into a real problem. I had a class of twelve students who had been studying with me for over a year and half. In one class I noticed that one student was tense and the group picked up his energy. I was in the middle of coaching an acting scene, but had trouble concentrating because of the uneasiness in the group. I stopped the coaching and asked the group, "What is going on? What are you feeling?" This student exploded and said, "You are too gentle. You are not tough enough on me. I want more things said about what is not working in my scene." My perception was that I was tough, with love, on my students.

So I checked it out with the other people in the group. One other student did want me to be tougher on him and more demanding. The other ten students thought I was tough enough for them. We spent about an hour discussing their feelings and it cleared the air. Had I not acknowledged what was going on, or the energy in the room, I think things would have gotten worse. Again, if I want my students to risk and take chances, I must be willing to do the same.

9. Miscellaneous problems

The chitter-chatterer or whisperer: When there is whispering or chitter-chatter between group members, I ask them to please respect the concentration needed for the work we do. Whispering and chitter-chatter is distracting. Please be considerate of each person working in the group. Groups need clear boundaries about what is tolerated and what is not tolerated. You, as a leader, must decide what you are comfortable with in your own groups.

The rambler: Occasionally during a feedback session you will have one person who rambles on and on. You can interrupt her and say, "What you are saying is wonderful, but can you sum it up in just a few sentences?" You don't want to rush the rambler, who may be collecting her thoughts as she speaks, but you do want to suggest that she focuses so she can express the essence of what she wants to say.

10. Problems that have no solutions

Occasionally, you will be faced with a problem that has no solution. You will rack your brains and nothing works. Example: Several years ago, I had one group that didn't mesh well together. They were all nice people and the work done in the group was good. However, they rarely asked questions and the group spirit was different from my other classes. I said, "I don't feel you're all really here for each other or are truly supportive of each other's work. I feel you're not paying attention when someone else is working." We talked about the situation and it seemed to get a little bit better. Yet, in my opinion, the group never totally bonded. I kept thinking, "What's wrong? What am I doing wrong? All the other classes I have taught have bonded. What should I do?" To this day, I still don't know what I could have done differently. The only answer I came up with was that the students basically didn't care about each other. They rarely came to class early to get to know each other and rarely went out together after a class for a cup of tea or a snack. Perhaps they were each dealing with their own lives and problems, but nothing I did seemed to bring the group together in a meaningful way.

My solution was to let it go. It did teach me a lesson. Never take anything for granted. Even though I had been teaching for eighteen years at that point, I was at a loss about how to handle it. Knowing that I must be aware, sensitive and vulnerable lets me see and appreciate my own fallibility and humanness.

Faith is the beginning of all good things.
— Buddha

Tips for Procedures

There are several categories under Procedures.
1. Time
2. Space
3. Communication within a group
4. Objectives and Sensitivity
5. Journals
6. Evaluations

If we are always arriving and departing, it is also true that we are eternally anchored.
One's destination is never a place, but rather a new way of looking at things.
— Henry Miller, writer

1. Time

These time samples are based on a three-hour class. We start with the *Relaxation Series* (p. 71) and *Energizing Series* (p. 75). After the series, participants ask questions or give feedback on the previous sessions. If you meet once a week, things may come up for participants that need clarification. They may also wish to share an experience that was valuable for them during the week. Here are some suggestions for time allotments you might allow for each type of exercise:

Group improvisations: 10-30 minutes
Two-people improvisations in front of the group: 2-3 minutes each
Three- to five-people improvisations in front of the group: 3-5 minutes each
Time when the groups go off on their own to work out an improvisation: 10-15 minutes
Symbolic drawing time: 5-10 minutes
Feedback sessions: 15-20 minutes

In Appendix F, you will find suggested times for each exercise. You are free to take any part of an exercise and fit it into whatever time frame you have.

Every day we are given stones. But what do we build? Is it a bridge or is it a wall?

— Anonymous

2. Space

The ideal space is a large room. Arrange the chairs in a circle or semi-circle. The circle symbolizes unity and equality. If your space is smaller, the chairs can be set up in a semi circle. You use the space in the front of the room as the stage or working area. The working area or stage should at the same level as the chairs. In other words, don't use a stage that's above the audience, like in a traditional theater. This sets up your participants to want to perform, which is not what this work is all about.

3. Communication within a group

People become excited doing these exercises. It's important to stress that there is no talking when others are working. During the feedback period, only one person talks at a time. I have worked with adults for thirty years and have seen many people interrupt each other. They don't mean to be rude. They can't contain their excitement and are bursting forth and wanting to share their insights and breakthroughs.

It's important to say, "When someone is finished talking, please don't jump in right away with what you want to say. Give them some time after they finish talking to take a breath and see if there's anything else they want to say. You don't want to rush each other. Sometimes the person speaking will take a pause, collect his thoughts and continue speaking. Please make sure that the person talking is finished before you speak."

If you genuinely love, or at least send kind thoughts to a thing, it will change before your eyes.

— John and Lynn St. Clair Thomas, writers

4. Objectives and Sensitivity

Plan objectives for each group meeting. Examples of objectives might be:

- To make members feel more comfortable with each other
- To give them an awareness of their body
- To work on being vulnerable
- To bring out the child in each person
- To give them certain skills in different areas. You decide what those areas are.

Always remember that the person is more important than your objectives and what you're teaching that day. You can easily switch an objective if something more important is happening within your group. The people must come first. I learned that lesson in an interesting way when I was twenty-five years old. I had just begun teaching and went to an astrologer. We had never met each other before. He said, "You are a teacher. You care a lot about what you teach, but sometimes the material you teach is more important to you than the people you are teaching. Always make sure the people come first." This comment changed my teaching forever. Always be sensitive to each person's needs and be open to revising your objectives and plan for the day.

I want to write, but more than that, I want to bring out all kinds of things that lie buried deep in my heart.
— Anne Frank

5. Journals

Journals are an effective way for you to keep in touch with each group member. Journal assignments can be made at every session and journals can be turned in every two or three weeks. In addition to keeping the assignments in the journals, each member can add questions, make comments and give feedback on a particular session. In this way the journal can be a kind of letter between you and the members of your group. If a member doesn't want a certain page or pages to be read, he can fold those pages in half. That will be your signal not to read those pages.

If you prefer, the journals don't have be turned in. In this case, stress the value of keeping a journal. I remember a person who had been in the group for a year said to me, "You know, I never started keeping a journal until the thirtieth week. I should have kept it much earlier. It's been incredibly valuable to me."

All limitations are self-imposed.
— John Foster Dulles, U.S. Secretary of State

6. Evaluations

At the end of your last group meeting, distribute a sheet on the work you have covered in the workshop and ask your members to write an evaluation. If you teach a one-day workshop, it is still valuable to distribute evaluations. Here are some suggestions for questions on the evaluations:

- What did you enjoy the most?
- What was most valuable?
- What suggestions do you have for improving the workshop?

- Self-evaluation: Write about how you think you did in the workshop, improvements, ways you have grown, ways you would like to grow more, where you would like to go in your work, ways you changed, any ways you feel blocked, challenges, and anything you would like to share with me. It's just as valuable for them to write the evaluation as it is for you to read it. For them, it will be a centering and clarifying process. Many people have asked me to send them a copy of their self-evaluation. They keep it and they can see on paper their reflections, their process and their growth over the course of our time together.

Read the evaluations carefully. As a line in *The King and I* says, "From your students you are taught." The participants in my groups have given me invaluable suggestions and ideas in their evaluations. I incorporate about 95% of their suggestions into my future teaching.

I hear and I forget. I see and I remember. I do and I understand.
— Confucius

Tips for Improvisations

Benefits of Improvisation

In many of the exercises, there are group improvisations where everyone participates. The definition of improvisation is 'a creation spoken or written or composed extemporaneously, without prior preparation.' In some of the improvisations, participants are divided into groups and can play extemporaneously with roles. That's the fun of improv—you are totally in the moment. Some of the benefits of improvisation are that it:

1. Inspires you to trust your creative impulses
2. Enhances your creativity and originality
3. Liberates your imagination and sense of humor even more
4. Increases your flexibility and spontaneity
5. Encourages you to take even more risks
6. Helps to get rid of your 'inner critic'
7. Inspires you to think outside of the box
8. Stimulates you to come up with new ideas and solutions
9. Excites you to live in the moment
10. Encourages you to find other parts of yourself

Tips on Coaching Improvisations

There are 11 major areas in coaching improvisations.

1. Defining objectives and actions
2. Say yes
3. The pace is set by you
4. You are the third eye
5. Keep the ball rolling
6. Spotlighting
7. Silences are good
8. No violence
9. Creating suspense
10. Avoiding stereotypes
11. Creating an autobiography

What we DO reveals who we are.
— Unknown

1. Defining Objectives and Actions

In most of the exercises, group members must have an objective and an action.

An *objective* is defined as one person wanting something from another person. It is a **need** that one person has from another person. Example: My objective is that I need to borrow $4,000 from you. Your objective **must always involve the other person**.

Many people have a difficult time with objectives because they have a hard time asking for what they want and need from another person. And that is **exactly** what they must do when they have an objective.

Don't be frustrated if your group doesn't understand objectives right away. Even after you define it and give examples, it may be challenging for each person to actually ask his partner for an objective. When they ask for what they want in the improvisation, they will also be learning how to ask for what they want in life.

An easy way for them to begin to understand objectives is to write a list of everything they want from someone as they go through a day or week in their life. Example: I needed to borrow Sam's car. I needed Ann to help me make supper. They bring their list into class and read to the group what they needed from people in a given day. Soon each participant will be going through his day, being aware of what he wants and needs from another person or group of people.

An *action* is a verb. It is the HOW you get your objective. It must be an *active verb*. I define an action as something you can **physically do to someone else**. You may do the action physically or you can do the action with the **tone** of your voice.

Example: My objective is that I want you to cook dinner tonight. My action could be: To stroke you, to smother you, to attack you, to dismember you. You just fill in the blank: To _____ you.

Actions must make you HOT to go. They must turn you on. In an improvisation, you can only act actions. You can't act ideas. I have each student bring in a list of one hundred actions. They can take that list from their own life, from watching television or by watching how other people GET what they want from another person. Either way, through self-observations or by watching others, they will see how powerful actions are. We try to get what we want in many ways. When one way isn't working, we try to get it another way and use different actions.

Example: I want you to clean the house for me. I embrace you. That doesn't work. I stroke you. That doesn't work. I hit you. That may work. I hit you, not physically, but with my voice. Tell your group to be aware of how many different ways people try to get what they want. It's fascinating. When an improvisation works, each person has a strong objective and action.

The possibilities of YES are always more interesting to act than the certainty of no.
— Michael Shurtleff, casting director and acting teacher

2. Say Yes

It is important to tell your groups that in improvisation, they **always** say "yes" when their partner makes them an offer. Example: "Would you like a cup of tea?"

"Yes."

"Would you like some cream and sugar?"

"Yes."

"May I put a bit of a spider in it for you?"

"Oh, yes!"

If you say no to your partner, the improvisation ends. A cardinal rule of improvisation is to always **say yes** to your partners and never to contradict them.

Example: A couple is on their honeymoon. The bride says to her groom, "Let's go swimming at 4 a.m. tomorrow morning. I remember your mother suggested that to us."

The groom can say, "Oh, my mother was a wild woman! That would be fantastic to go swimming at 4 a.m.!"

If the groom said, "My mother never said that," the improvisation would end and the players would be at a standstill. Always say YES.

Be not afraid of growing slowly. Be afraid only of standing still.
— Chinese proverb

3. The pace is set by you

When you assign an improvisation, your excitement starts the improvisation on an upbeat note. The energy and pace of the group is set by you. When you need volunteers for a two- to four-person improvisation, some people will be excited about volunteering. On the other hand, you might find that when you ask for volunteers, the entire group sits there and no one makes a move. So, what do you do?

You pick people at random with a twinkle in your eye. You go up to each person and escort him or her into the playing area and say, "You, you and you. Good, let's start."

Or, after you pick each person, you can quickly give them the outline of the improvisation- who they are, where they are, and their objective. You give the directions secretly to the participants doing the improvisation. The rest of your group **doesn't hear what you're saying and this creates excitement for everyone**. The audience has no idea what will happen in the scene. Example: To one person you whisper, "You own a beauty shop and want to convince the man who enters your shop to get his head shaved."

To the second person you whisper, "You're late for an appointment and just want a quick hair trim." Say, "Curtain," and the scene begins.

If you want to stop the action, you say, "Freeze." This means they stop and hold their body in a frozen position. You give the next set of directions and then say, "Begin," and the improvisation continues.

To travel hopefully is better than to arrive.

— Sir James Jeans, British physicist and astronomer

4. You are the third eye

It's important that you stay on the outside and watch the improvisations as you coach them. You shouldn't be a part of the scene. The participants will feel safer knowing there is an outside eye watching them. You need to be aware of each person and what is going on inside of them, so you can jump in at any time and restructure the scene, if necessary.

You may need to end an improvisation if a situation develops that could be threatening to someone in the group. Being the third eye, you say to the group, "I am invisible. I might come up to you during the scene and whisper something in your ear. I might give you a new objective or create a conflict. I might tell you to pick someone's pockets or start an argument with someone." When you function as the third eye, you're the overseer and can give your students an idea that keeps the ball rolling.

I see my life as an unfolding set of opportunities to awaken.

— Ram Dass

5. Keep the ball rolling

There are several ways to keep the ball rolling in improvisational work. When the ball is dropped, participants are at a loss as to what to do. If a scene is not working well, here are several suggestions.

1. As was suggested, you can be the third eye and be invisible. You whisper a new objective or action in a member's ear to raise the stakes and make the action move ahead.

2. Give a new focus. Say, "Freeze. Think of a color and continue the scene being the essence of that color, in movement as well as with your voice." Or you can say, "Change your rhythm. Think of one of your favorite musical tunes and let that tune run through your body as you continue the scene. If it is silently inside you, it will affect your movement and voice."

3. You can combine two exercises. Example: If you are doing *Elements: Earth-Air-Fire-Water* (p. 119) you can add the exercise called *Movement Qualities* (p. 101). Once you have read over all of the exercises, you'll have a better sense of how you might want to combine them.

4. Say, "Freeze. Do a speed run." This means that each member in the scene moves and talks as fast as they can. It may get a bit crazy, but this technique picks up the group energy and gets people out of their heads so they're not thinking about the scene.

Any of these suggestions will add new dimensions and energy to the work.

The art of acting is making the other person important to you.
— Unknown

6. Spotlighting

Spotlighting is essential when teaching improvisation. Spotlighting is learning how to give and 'take stage.' If four people are doing an improvisation, all four people can't talk at once. If they do, the audience won't hear a thing and it will be confusing to them. An audience must know where to focus their attention during a scene, where to look and who to listen to. It's like a spotlight is on two people in the scene.

Two of the people in the scene must tone down their conversation and lower their voices. By one couple talking softly, the audience can focus on the two people who are talking. Then the two in the spotlight can tone down their conversation and the two people who were quieter can raise the volume of their conversation so the spotlight goes over to them. The people in the spotlight 'take stage.' They are the ones who the audience is focusing upon.

Spotlighting is learning how to share the space with the other people in your scene. The reason spotlighting is important is that it teaches people to be sensitive to each other, to give and take, to create an ensemble and to share the space with each other. Even in a three-person scene, people must spotlight. In improvisation, there is no director. Each person takes responsibility to give and take with his fellow players.

To be eloquent is to be most silent.
— Unknown

7. Silences are good

Let your group know that they don't always have to be talking in a scene. People are terrified of silent moments, so they often babble. Tell them, "Take your time. In life, we take pauses, as we speak. Silences are real. They're a part of a natural conversation. A lot can happen in a silence. If you have a silence, and can't think of anything to say, TRUST that something will come. It always does." It adds to the suspense if there is silence. You could do a demonstration of this technique.

There is another way to illustrate the point that in normal conversation there are silences. Ask two people to go in front of the group. Each one sits in a chair. Ask them to have a conversation about what they did yesterday. The group will see how many silences occur in their conversation. Or you might ask someone to tell about a wonderful moment in her life. We all need time to pause, reflect, and see and feel the memory before we verbalize it.

The only way to have peace is to teach peace. By teaching peace you must learn it yourself.
— A Course in Miracles

8. No violence

Violence is never allowed in improvisations. This must be stated categorically. In my first year of teaching, one person almost did a karate chop on another person. No one was hurt, but from that day on, I never took anything for granted as a group leader. Always state this ground rule clearly.

The most beautiful thing we can experience is the mysterious.
— Albert Einstein

9. Creating suspense

When you're doing improvisations, it takes a moment to whisper into one person's ear an objective or action. You don't want the whole group to hear what you whisper. It's a secret. This creates suspense and anticipation of what's going to happen. The group wonders what you told each person. Each person in the scene wonders what you whispered to the other people.

To a true artist only that face is beautiful which,
quite apart from its exterior, shines with the truth within the soul.
— Mahatma Gandhi

10. Avoiding stereotypes

Avoid stereotypes when assigning roles. Example: You might ask a woman to be a truck driver and a man to be a secretary, a woman to be a plumber and a man to be a manicurist. This allows for interesting situations to develop and helps avoid gender-role stereotyping.

In many of the exercises, participants are asked to choose a character to play. Many of the characters they pick will be stereotyped as: a rich lady, a bum, and an athlete. Make sure you ask them three to five of the *Autobiographical Questions for Characters* (p. 219). This process will help to ground their characters and avoid superficiality.

When you withdraw all your energy from the past and future,
a tremendous explosion happens. That explosion is creativity.
— Bhagwan Shree Rajneesh, Indian mystic, guru and philosopher

Beginning Exercises

Opening Exercise for Your Group
30-45 minutes

PURPOSE: Gives each person a clear image of what he wants to receive during the group/workshop
Creates a bond between participants

TOOLS: Drawing board, a foam core board is light
Sheet of paper, 18" x 24" or smaller
Crayons and markers

Notes to the Leader

This exercise is invaluable for you and your group. It's a wonderful diagnostic tool and gives you important information about the participants, their needs and their expectations from the group. By knowing their needs, you can assist each person in clarifying and achieving what he or she wants from the group experience. As they share their drawings, they bond with each other.

Each person has a foam core board and a sheet of newsprint on top of it. It's fun to dump a bag of crayons and markers in the center of the circle and ask each person to pick whatever colors they like. Their drawing tools are in front of them. They can sit at large tables or spread out on the floor. Everyone should have plenty of room around themselves to draw and enter into their own world as they do this exercise.

Procedure

Please sit up straight in your chairs, or if you're on the floor, please center yourself by sitting up straight. Let your hands rest by your side. Close your eyes and focus on your breathing. Breathe in and out through your nose. Or breathe anyway that's calm and relaxing for you. This exercise is done in silence. Trust the first image that comes to you. What would you like to receive during the group/retreat/weekend/class? What do you need? Get an image and draw it on the newsprint. Please use your non-dominant hand as your draw. If you are right-handed, draw with your left hand. If you are left-handed, draw with your right hand. See page 30 for why we draw with our non-dominant hand.

Notes to the Leader

You, too, can draw what you'd like to receive. The fact that you are drawing and sharing in the first exercise will encourage your group to be more open and vulnerable. Usually, you're not participating in the exercises, but in this one, it's wonderful if you do. As you sense the drawings are being finished, you say to your group, "You might want to make notes on the back of your drawings or in your journal as you finish your drawings."

The reason you say this AFTER their drawings are completed, is that if you say it too early on, they might focus on writing rather than drawing. You want them to plunge right into symbolic drawing at the first meeting.

Feedback Session

Depending on the size of your group, you say, "Let's share our drawings. Hold your drawing up and say anything you'd like us to know about it. Each person will have about two minutes."

If your group is more than twelve people, they find a partner, someone they don't know. People can take three minutes to share something about their drawing with the other person. After they're finished, you say, "Let's all come together and if anyone would like to share anything they learned, that would be wonderful. When you give your drawing voice, it grounds your experience even more." In closing this exercise you say, "Save your drawings. You're welcome to hang them up in your home. Sometimes just seeing your drawing during the period that you're in the class, can make what you want, happen."

Be yourself. Everyone else is already taken.

— Oscar Wilde

My Name Is
30-45 minutes

PURPOSE: Breaks the ice
Increases vulnerability
Breaks down barriers between people
Creates group ensemble

Notes to the Leader

I use this exercise at every first class meeting. It's one of my favorite exercises, since it creates group ensemble immediately. It allows everyone to be vulnerable and feel silly at the same time. I teach the exercise in many different ways. I might ask them to do it as a child, or a quality they love most in themselves, or do it as quality that they would like to bring into their life, and so on. It teaches the group to connect, be vulnerable, share, be in the moment, be aware of themselves and other people, and so much more.

It's important to do this exercise at your first group meeting because members make personal contact with each person in the group and this creates the group ensemble and SAFETY in your group. One of the most important things I teach is to be vulnerable and to take risks. That is what this exercise accomplishes. If participants take several of the workshops I teach, they would this exercise at every first meeting. There are many ways to do this exercise.

Procedure

Let's make a huge circle and sit on the floor. (If you have an older group who can't sit on the floor, they can sit in chairs.) If someone wants to sit in a chair, let's make that person in the chair a part of our circle.

I'd like each one of you, one at a time to say your name to each person in the group. You can stay where you are or move. That's up to you. Remember, there is no right or wrong way to do this exercise. Make sure you say your name to each person in the group. All you say is, "Hi, my name is _____," and then you can move on to the next person. You don't engage in conversation. You say your name and then go on to the next person, until you've connected with each person in the group.

To those of us watching the exercise, please pay attention as each person does this exercise. This is your first observation assignment. A person's shoulders and back are the most expressive part of his body, so if a person isn't facing you, it doesn't matter.

Close your eyes. Get an image of yourself as a child. You are five to ten years old. You'll say your name to each person as you, being a five to ten year old. Open your eyes and let's begin. Remember, there is no right or wrong way to do this exercise.

Occasionally, depending on the group I am leading, I might add, "This exercise is challenging because I am asking you to really LOOK at another person and share who you are with that person. Jumping right into this exercise forces you to be in the moment and lets you be spontaneous and creative."

Feedback Session

Ask your group how they felt doing the exercise. Allow time for their feedback, before you ask the following questions.

1. Feelings: How did you feel doing it?
2. Observation: What did you notice?
3. Approaching: How did it feel to approach each person?
4. Relaxation: When did you feel most relaxed?
5. Tension: Did you feel tense?
6. Connection: Did you connect with the person you said your name to? Did you look each person in the eye? Did you let the other person in? Were you in the moment and present? Did you send out and receive positive energy? What was your relationship like?
7. Space: What was the space like between you? What was your special relationship? Was there too much space or too little space between you?
8. Voice: What happened to your voice? Was it relaxed or tense?
9. Your Process: What was the process you went though like when you were waiting for your turn? Did you try to plan ahead on how you would do the exercise? Were you judging yourself as you did the exercise?
10. Touch: Did you feel comfortable about touching each person? Often a connection can be made by touching someone. An example would be in a job interview. When you shake hands with the person interviewing you, you pick up energy from the other person. It can also relax you to shake hands. Try it the next time you are in a new situation and see what happens. It can break the ice between people. You can also touch people with your voice in a caring way.
11. Your body: What happened inside your body? What did you notice? How was your breathing?
12. Levels: Did you sit down with people or look down at them as you stood up? It doesn't matter what you did. Just be aware of levels when you meet and are talking to people.
13. Eye contact: Did you make eye contact? Did you let the other person in or did you put up a wall?
14. Rhythms: What was your rhythm? What was the rhythm of the other person?

15. Sub-personality: Did you experience a different part of yourself, a different sub-personality? What was it like? Did you surprise yourself?

16. Impulses: Did you act on your impulses or did you censor yourself? Did you find yourself thinking and figuring out HOW to do the exercise? Did you judge it? Remember, judgment kills creativity. Trust your impulses.

17. Take time: Did you take time and finish with each person you said your name to, or did you rush around the circle? Again, it doesn't matter what you did. Just be aware of how you did the exercise. Did you wait a beat and complete the interaction before you went on to the next person? Did you feel finished before you went on to the next person?

18. Good energy: Did you radiate good energy to each person as you went around the circle?

19. Breathing: Did you remember to breathe during the exercise or were you holding your breath?

20. Thinking: Were you thinking as you went to each person? Were you spontaneous and able to let yourself act on how you felt in the moment?

21. Sharing yourself: Did you feel comfortable in sharing who you are?

22. Body change: To have an image is to have a body change. Any image you have in your body will change the way you use your body and voice. So when I said, "Be a child," you had an image and it changed how you used your body and voice.

Variations

Say your name to each person in the following way.

1. Express the essence of who you are
2. With total acceptance of the other person
3. With a quality you love in yourself
4. Asking the question, "What do I want this person to know about me?"
5. The way you choose to be with that person RIGHT NOW
6. The way you most want to be in your life right now
7. Pretend that person is an old friend whom you haven't seen in a long time
8. With a sense of total GIVING to that person
9. With a sense of total RECEIVING from that person
10. Your favorite part of nature you would most like to be and communicate that part to each person
11. A part of yourself that you exaggerate and blow up
12. With the premise that 'the art of acting is making the other person important to you'
13. A different part of yourself that you usually don't share when you first meet someone
14. A five-year-old child

15. An inanimate object
16. A gesture that expresses your essence
17. Non-verbally using only movement to express your name and essence
18. Be as silly as you can
19. What does the other person bring out in you when you look at her?
20. Say your name as if time has stopped for ten seconds
21. Radiating love
22. Your favorite mood
23. Bring totally present
24. How you want the person you are saying your name to feel

Assignment

In everyday life, introduce yourself to someone and use the *My Name Is* exercise. Example: You can do it with total acceptance and sending positive energy.

Say your name to three new people you meet this week and see how it feels. See what it feels like to use some of the techniques you experienced in this exercise. These people could be a person working in a store, the usher at the movie, anyone you don't know. We will share our experiences next week.

He that can take rest is greater than he that can take cities.

— Benjamin Franklin

Relaxation Series
10-15 minutes

PURPOSE: Relaxes body tension

Energizes and centers body energy

Relaxes your group so people are in the present moment

Centers the group leader so you are in the present moment

Notes to the Leader

This series is given during the first fifteen minutes of each class meeting. People come to a class in various states of stress, upset, weariness and excitement. It's crucial to relax each person's mind and body so your group is ready to play, work and create together.

Use a tone of voice that's calming and soothing as you take your group through the Relaxation Series. If your group can't lie on the floor, they can sit in chairs.

Procedure

Find your own space on the floor. Take off your shoes if you like. Lie down on your back. Close your eyes. Bend your knees and if you have any lower back issues or you want to relax your lower back even more. Let your body sink into the floor. Feel each part of your body touching the floor. Take in any sounds you hear in the room or outside of the room. Let all sounds into your consciousness. Don't block anything out. You can as easily do this Relaxation Series in Times Square as in your own quiet place. Make sure you are breathing in and out through your mouth and your nose. Your lips, tongue and jaw are relaxed. Your mouth is open slightly. Feel your belly rising and falling.

Head

Slowly turn your head from side to side. Let your jaw relax. Your head should be moving so slowly that if I were to look at you, I should hardly see it moving.

Arms

Stretch your right arm perpendicular to your body. Make a tight fist and try to touch the ceiling with your fist. Stretch your right arm up to the ceiling and then let it fall loosely to the floor. The relaxation is just as important as the stretching.

Relax the rest of your body as you are stretching each body part. Stretch your left arm up to the ceiling and then let it fall loosely to the floor.

Legs

Stretch your right leg about two inches off the floor. Stretch it all the way from your hip. Release. Stretch your left leg. Release.

Buttocks

Clench your buttocks tightly. Or as a dance teacher once said to our class, "Squeeze your peaches together." Hold that squeeze and release. Do this three times.

Shoulders

Turn your shoulders in toward your chest bone. Hold them tightly. Release. Do this three times.

Body Stretch

Do a full body stretch. Pretend two people are pulling you from either end. Stretch as far as you can in both directions. Release. Relax your whole body. Feel your breath going in and out.

Liquid

Imagine a liquid is being poured into the top of your head. It's a very pleasant sensation. Be aware of the liquid's color, weight and texture as it fills up the inside of your head. It's a very pleasant sensation as it goes down through your head and into your neck and shoulders. It goes down through your arms, relaxing each part of your arm. Let part of the liquid trickle out through each finger. The rest of the liquid goes slowly down into your chest and waist, hips and thighs. It continues down your body and relaxes each part of your body that it touches. It goes into your calves and your feet and trickles slowly out your toes. It circles under the floor that you are lying on and begins again in the top of your head. This time, take the liquid at your own pace, letting it relax each part of your body that it touches. Let the liquid gather at one point and flow down your body and go out through your toes. Again, feel your breath going in and out. Let your body feel very light, as if it were floating on a piece of chiffon. Or let it feel very heavy as if it was sinking into the ground.

Sitting Position

Find the easiest way to come to a sitting position. Roll over onto your side in a prenatal state and then slowly come to a sitting position. Use the least amount of effort to come to a sitting position.

Vertebral Roll

Slowly come to a standing position doing a vertebral roll. Let each vertebrae unwind as you come to a standing position. Now we'll do a vertebral roll down to the floor. To do a vertebral roll, lower your chin to your chest very slowly. Try to see each vertebrae in your neck moving as you lower your chin to your chest. Slowly go down toward the floor. Bend your knees slightly so you don't put any pressure on your lower back. Go down towards the floor only as far as is comfortable for you. Slowly roll up. Leave your eyes closed. Come back to a standing position.

Energy

Feel the energy coming up through the earth into your feet, up into your legs, into your chest and out the top of your head. Feel energy radiating from each part of your body. Feel that there is an aura around your entire body and this aura is radiating out and filling the whole room and going beyond. Slowly open your eyes.

The body says what words cannot.
— Martha Graham, dancer and choreographer

Energizing Series
5 minutes

PURPOSE: Relaxes body tension
Energizes and centers body energy
Relaxes your group so people are in the present moment
Centers the group leader so you are in the present moment

Procedure

We add sound so that the voice is energized and warmed up at the same time as the body. The energizing series gets your body all warmed up, energized and ready to go.

Head

Stand up straight and nod YES with your head. Let your head fall back and then drop forward. Relax your jaw so that when your head is back, your jaw and mouth is open. Voice an open "AH" sound as you drop your head forward and back. Do this three times. Now move your head from side to side in a NO motion. Say "MA MA MA MA MA MA," as you turn your head from side to side. Make sure that you look at one point on one wall and then when you turn your head the other way, look at a specific point on the other wall. When you focus on one point, you won't get dizzy. Say "MA MA," as you turn your head from side to side. Do this three times. Combine both head movements. Say YES with your head and then NO with your head. Let your head fall back, forward and side to side. Add the sounds "AH AH, MA MA MA MA".

Shoulders

Move your shoulders in a circle. Lift them up toward your ears, back, down and forward. Circle your shoulders and add the sound "WA WA WA WA," as you roll your shoulders. Reverse the direction of your shoulder roll. Lift your shoulders up, forward, down and back. Add the sound "OH LA LA OO LA LA," as you roll your shoulders.

Rib Cage

Move your rib cage from one side to the other side. Move it from right to left, left to right. Do this motion slowly.

Notes to the Leader

The best way to teach the rib cage exercise is to have your group sit on the floor, so their fannies are not moving. Tell them to move their rib cage slowly from one side to the other. This movement is very small. If they practice this at home, they will be able to isolate the rib cage.

Hips

Bend your knees slightly and swing your hips from side to side. Add the sound "WEE WAY WHY WEE WAY WHY." Move your hips in a circle. Bend your knees and push your hips forward, to the side, to the back and to the other side. Add the sound "OO MA MA OO MA MA." Write your name with your hips. Make sure you dot your i's and cross your t's. Draw a figure eight with your hips and say "Round the rugged rock the ragged rascal ran."

Jumping

We'll do ten jumps in the air. Stand in a ballet first position with your heels touching to form a V and your feet pointed out. Make sure you bend your knees so when you land you don't hurt your Achilles tendon. Let your arms swing forward in a circle as you jump. Keep your body centered as you jump and everyone yell, "WHOOPEE, WHOOPEE, WHOOPEE!" Relax.

I suspect that the most basic and powerful way to connect with another person is to listen. Just listen. Perhaps the most important thing we can ever give each other is our attention. And especially if it's given from the heart.
— Rachel Naomi Remen, M.D., author, educator and medical reformer

Listening Exercise
30-45 minutes

PURPOSE: Increases and improves listening skills
Develops concentration
Breaks the ice
Heightens awareness of other people's ideas and feelings
Builds sensitivity

Notes to the Leader

This is one of the most valuable exercises I teach to groups. It's best to do this exercise in the first or second meeting.

Procedure

Divide into groups of three or four people. Find people you don't know. Each group should sit in a separate area of the room, so you have space and privacy. You don't want to be able to hear what the other groups are saying. I'll give each group a subject to discuss. Everyone in the group will be able to contribute to the discussion. Each person in the group will express his or her ideas and views on the subject. The other people in the group can NOT interrupt you or ask you questions. One person talks at a time. Each person can talk for two to three minutes. Then a second person in your group will respond to what the first person said. BUT, before the second person states his opinions, he must FIRST repeat the ESSENCE of what the first person said.

If the second person doesn't repeat the essence of what the first person said, the first person can say, "No, that isn't really what I said. This is what I said." And then the first person repeats the essence of what he said. The second person tries again to repeat the essence of what the first person said. It is CRUCIAL that the person repeat the essence of what the person who spoke before him said, before they state their own views and opinions. BE HONEST WITH EACH OTHER. If the person after you isn't really repeating the essence of what you said, don't by shy about saying to him that what he said was incorrect. Each person doesn't have to say the WHOLE of what was said, only the essence. It takes about forty-five seconds to a minute to repeat the essence.

If three people have spoken, you don't need to repeat the essence of the first and second person. You need only repeat the essence of what the person who spoke immediately before you.

Notes to the Leader

You can pick any current topics that would be of interest to everyone in your group. The subjects I have used in the past are: Does the men's movement or women's movement affect you in any way? What don't you like about being a man? What don't you like about being a woman? Discuss how you feel about being a man or a woman. This topic is exciting because it brings up feelings and opens participants to their vulnerability. Ask your group to share something about themselves as they speak. In this way, people will be getting to know each other and, at the same time, they'll be doing the exercise.

You can give each group twenty minutes and let each person talk for two minutes. It's easy to chime in and say, "Move on to the second person, if you haven't moved on yet."

Feedback Session

How did it feel? What did you notice? What did it feel like when someone repeated the essence of what you had said? How many of you were planning what you were going to say and didn't listen to what the person next to you was saying?

Notes to the Leader

You can point out the benefits of doing the Listening Exercise.

1. It is a wonderful therapeutic technique. People feel HEARD when you repeat the essence and therefore, open up to you even more. They feel appreciated.

2. By repeating the essence, you make sure that you understood what the person said to you. Often a person repeats the essence and the person says, "Yes, that is what I said, but that's not what I MEANT." You help the person figure out what he REALLY meant to say.

3. You may find that when you repeat what you think the person meant, you pick up on his non-verbal behavior and cues. The person may say to you, "That is not what I said to you, but that is exactly what I feel and what I meant to say. How did you know?" You read his body language. You have listened with your eyes, ears and heart.

Assignment

Try this exercise three times this week. When you are having a conversation with someone, try repeating the essence of what they say. See what happens to the quality of your interaction. Bring the results and feedback to our next group meeting.

Notes to the Leader

Don't forget to ask the group the following week what happened when they did this exercise. You'll hear wonderful success stories. It will support each person even more in trying this exercise outside of classes as well as within your group.

When I taught workshops for physicians, we did the exercise in pairs. These physicians learned how much they listen or don't listen to their patients. Many physicians let me know months later, that this exercise changed the way they practice medicine.

With the physicians, I have them share with a partner, something they're looking forward to in their life. They go back and forth with their partner several times, but they always must repeat the essence of what they hear before responding with their event. Then I have them take three minutes apiece and share some challenge they are facing in their lives. Again, they must repeat the essence of their partner's challenge before responding with their own thoughts.

Motion creates emotion.
— Ted Shawn, dancer and choreographer

Finding Your Center
30-45 minutes

PURPOSE: Increases body awareness

Teaches participants observational skills

Encourages participants to be silly and laugh at themselves

Bonds the group

Notes to the Leader

Stress to your group that it doesn't matter what their physical center is. Participants can become critical of themselves and think, "I wonder if I should change my center. Why do I lead with my hips?" Make sure they understand that we all move in certain ways and there is no best way to walk down the street. Be positive in this exercise and not psychological. Don't try to figure out why people walk as they do. Otherwise, participants will feel self-conscious.

Procedure

You all lead with a certain body part when you walk. Your center is where your energy emanates from. It may be in your forehead, nose, chin, chest, hips, and so on. Some people lead with an extraverted center. Example: Your chest might stick way out as you walk. Or you can lead with an introverted center. Introverted means that a part of your body may cave in. Example: Your chest may be sunken as you walk. There is no right or wrong way to walk. We are going to see where your body center is.

I'd like everyone to gather at one end of the room. Each person will walk in a large circle around the room. You'll say what you think each person leads with when he walks. As you watch people, notice where their energy is, as they walk. It's not necessarily what body part comes first. It is where the energy is that PULLS the person forward. People can lead with the following body parts: forehead, nose, chin, chest, belly, hips, upper leg, knee, lower leg, and feet. Or their energy may not be within their body. It can be about six inches above their head. This gives the impression that they're light and almost floating through space. Their center may be introverted which is tucked in, or extraverted, which means that the body part is sticking out. There's no right or wrong way to walk. We're just noticing how people move. It's all good.

Notes to the Leader

As each person takes a turn, you might see two people who lead with their hips. You ask them to walk around the circle TOGETHER and have the group notice how they are walking ALIKE. Then again, although they might both lead with the same body part, their energy can be very different. Example: Someone might lead with his chest and have a very light and airy walk. The other person might also lead with their chest and have a heavy walk. It's fun to match people up who lead with the SAME body part, or who lead with DIFFERENT body parts. You might match up a person who leads with his forehead and someone who leads with his feet. The difference in the two people will be accentuated because your group will be seeing them walk together.

Procedure

Now that each person has had a turn, I'd like you all to get a taste of what it's like to move with each body center. Let's make a large circle.

Walk around the room leading with an extraverted forehead. What kind of person walks like this? What profession? (The people in your group will call out different professions and you can repeat what they say, so everyone hears it)

A professor? A nosey person? Freeze.

Lead with an extraverted nose. What kind of person leads with an extraverted nose? Freeze. Lead with an extraverted chest. How does this feel? Freeze. Lead with extraverted hips. What kind of people lead with extraverted hips. Freeze. Lead with an extraverted belly. Do you feel fat or thin? Freeze. Lead with extraverted upper legs. Freeze. Lead with extraverted knees. What kind of people lead with extraverted knees? Freeze. Lead with extraverted lower legs. Freeze. Lead with extraverted feet. Feel all of your energy coming from your feet. Freeze. Close our eyes. We'll go through all the body parts but this time move as if each body part is *introverted* (forehead, nose, chin, chest, and so on).

Freeze. Now close your eyes. Imagine that all your weight is leaving your body. Your body center is about six inches above your head. You have no body weight in your body. Open your eyes. Begin to move. How do you feel? What kind of person moves like this?

Two-Person Improvisation

I will pick two people and give them each an objective and an action. These people will pick the body center they want to lead with. The group will guess what that center is. You'll each get a turn. (See Appendix B for ideas for two-person improvisations.)

Notes to the Leader

You can tell each person what body center you want them to lead with. If you have a 'chest person', you might have them lead with their feet. Give them a body center other than what they don't normally lead with.

Feedback Session

How did this feel? What did you notice as you watched each person walk? What was each person leading with? How did what they lead with affect the rest of their body? How did the body center affect your voices?

Variation 1

Each person will walk around the room and we all imitate this person's walk and energy. We are not making fun of this person. We're just following him and 'becoming' him. See what you notice as we do this exercise.

Variation 2

Find someone in the group whose walk and energy is totally opposite from yours. Pair up and imitate each other. We'll watch each couple imitate each other. If you have an uneven number of people in your group, you can have one group with three people in it. They can take turns imitating each other.

Assignment

Follow five people this week and notice what center they lead with when they walk. You'll never be bored waiting for a bus again. It's fascinating to imagine what their life is like by how they walk.

It's fun to follow people discreetly and 'become' them. You can tell what people are like when you walk like they do. You begin to experience what they are feeling inside their body, when you walk as they do.

You cannot teach a man anything. You can only help him to find it within himself.

— Galileo Galilei

Slow Motion
15-30 minutes

PURPOSE: To gain body-awareness
To experience the subtleties of movement

Procedure

It's important that we understand how our bodies move. In this exercise, you'll feel each part of your body. Find a space in the room where you have plenty of room around you.

Find a point at the opposite end of the room. Focus on that point. Slowly move your body toward that point. You are moving so slowly that if I were to look at you, I should hardly be able to tell you are moving.

Notice what you have to do when you shift weight to take a step. Notice your balance. Notice every little movement you must make to propel yourself forward.

What does it feel like to move slowly? Where is your weight? Notice how you have to transfer weight to move ahead.

Feedback Session

What did you notice? How did you feel? Could you feel every muscle moving as you moved ahead? What new awareness do you have?

Your imagination is your preview of life's coming attractions.

— Albert Einstein

Drawing Exercise
30-45 minutes

PURPOSE: Inspires risk taking
Encourages spontaneity

TOOLS: Drawing utensils, crayons and markers
One sheet of newsprint or drawing paper
Foam core board to draw on

Notes to the Leader

Stress that being an artist is not important when you draw. You want their drawings to be child-like and innocent.

Procedure

Spread out in the room. Lie down and close your eyes. Get an image of anything at all. It can be a beautiful place, a color, a person, or an animal. Trust the first image you have. Open your eyes and draw your image. Use your non-dominant hand when you draw. If you are right handed, use your left hand and if you are left handed, use your right hand. See page 30 for why we draw with our opposite hand.

Movement

Stand up and become your drawing. Become whatever part of your drawing you choose. Move to its rhythm, colors, textures and symbolism. Personify your drawing in movement.

Group Improvisation

You're on an ocean liner. You came for a holiday and relaxation. Be the essence of your drawing on the ocean liner. You can talk to other people or remain quiet. Keep the essence of your drawing with you as you move and relate to others.

Feedback Session

What was it like for you become the essence of your drawing? Let's share our drawings and talk about the qualities you became in terms of movement. What was it like for you to be on the ocean liner? What part of the exercise worked best for you?

Variation

Do the same exercise, but this time in the group improvisation, don't talk to anyone else. Keep the essence of your drawing inside your body. Using a scale of one to ten, tone down the essence to a three. Now move it up the scale to an eight. Now bring the essence to a one. See if you feel the essence of your drawing stronger in your body when you don't talk. When you do this exercise non-verbally, it can affect your movement in different ways.

Habit is habit, and not to be flung out the window, but coaxed downstairs a step at a time.
— Mark Twain

Movement Traits
30-60 minutes

PURPOSE: Enhances self-awareness
Encourages play
Increases movement vocabulary

Notes to the Leader

This is a basic movement exercise where your group can begin to feel comfortable moving their bodies. They can experiment with new ways of being and start to become comfortable with being silly.

Procedure

Find your own space in the room. I'd like you to do each of the movement traits that I'll call out to you. You can move one body part and then add more parts as the movement goes through your body. Be respectful of each other's space.

Thrusting	Twisting	Darting	Pushing	Flowing	Striking	Flopping
Swaying	Slashing	Jumping	Rocking	Stretching	Leaping	Trotting
Shaking	Expanding	Bouncing	Folding	Pulling	Squeezing	Galloping
Collapsing	Flying					

Feedback Session

How did this feel? What did you notice?

Notes to the Leader

You can coach your group in various ways.
1. Move forward, backward, to the left, to the right. Move high, move low. Use different levels in your movement.
2. Be different animals as you do each movement.
3. Do silly activities that involve these movements.
4. Make sounds as you do the movement. See how the sound influences the movement or the movement influences and changes the sound.

Only from the heart can you touch the sky.
— Jalal ad-Din Rumi, Persian poet and mystic

Music Exercise
30-60 minutes

PURPOSE: Encourage inner life to come out
Develops awareness of rhythms

Notes to the Leader

You can either bring in a piece of music or ask someone in your group to bring in his favorite piece of music.

Procedure

I'm going to play a piece of music. Find a comfortable place to lie down and close your eyes. How does the music make you feel? What colors do you see? What images come to mind? What textures do you feel as the music plays? Get an image of a character or person that would match this music. Put clothes on the person. Create an autobiography. (See Appendix E)

Group Improvisation

You're in an ice cream parlor. You can be a customer, waiter or waitress. Keep the essence of the piece of music you just heard. Talk to other people in the parlor. Freeze. Close your eyes.

I'm going to play the music again. Find an image that is opposite to what the music brings up for you. What kind of person would go against the grain of this music? Feel this type of person enter your body.

Group Improvisation

You're in an antiques store. I'll appoint three salespeople. Keep the essence of the person you've just created who goes against the grain of the music. You can talk to other people or remain quiet.

Feedback Session

Did the images come easily to you as you listened to the music? What images did you have as you heard the music? What were the qualities of the first character you created? What were the qualities of the character you created that went against the grain of the music?

Imagination – its limits are only those of the mind itself.
                                        — Rod Serling, screenwriter

Color Exercise: Verbal
30-60 minutes

PURPOSE: Increases movement vocabulary
Develops appreciation of gestures
Illustrates how an image can influence your voice
Develops risk-taking

Notes to the Leader

Suggest to your group that they use their voices gently so they don't create vocal tension.

Procedure

Spread out in the room and close your eyes. Go with the first image you receive. I will be giving certain directions and follow your instincts and impulses as you hear the words.

Movement

What is your most favorite color? Open your eyes. Be that color in movement. Move around the room. Don't relate to anyone else. Add sound to your movement. You can relate to other people in the room. Let the sound of your color reach the people you meet. Try to communicate the sound of your color to different people. Start first with the movement and then add sound. Let that color fill your body. What is its rhythm and energy? How does the sound affect your gestures? How does this color affect your voice? Freeze. Close your eyes.

What is your least favorite color? Open your eyes. Be that color in movement. You can start with the sound first or begin with the movement. Don't relate to anyone else. How is the movement different than when you were your favorite color? How does this color affect your voice? Freeze. Close your eyes.

Be a hot color. Let this color start with your voice first and then go inside your body. What does this color do to your movement? Freeze. Close your eyes.

Be a cool color. How is your movement different than when you were the hot color? How does this color affect your voice? Move as this cool color.

Feedback Session

How did you feel? What did you notice happened to your body when you became each color? How was your energy different as you moved to each color? How did being different colors affect your voice?

Group Improvisation

You are at a funeral. Pick your most favorite color and be that color at the funeral. The improvisation is verbal. Feel the essence of that color inside your body. Notice how the color affects your voice.

Assignment

Take thirty minutes this week and go out in public and be one color. See how it affects your interactions with other people. Go to a neighborhood where you don't live, so you won't run into people you know. Take notes in your journal and plan to share your experiences in the next session.

Gazing on beautiful things acts on my soul, which thirsts for heavenly light.
— Michelangelo

Color Exercise: Non-Verbal
30-60 minutes

PURPOSE: Increases movement vocabulary
Develops appreciation of gestures
Develops risk-taking

Procedure

This exercise is non-verbal. It is done in silence. Spread out in the room and close your eyes. Go with the first image you receive. Follow your impulses and have fun with this exercise. What is your most favorite color? Open your eyes. Be that color in movement. Move any way you wish so you are expressing that one color in movement. Let that color fill your whole body. Don't relate to anyone else. What are your color's rhythm, energy, and pulse? What does this color to your gestures and your rhythm? Freeze. Close your eyes.

What is your least favorite color? Open your eyes. Be that color in movement. How do you move? What is your energy like now? How is the movement different than when you were your most favorite color? Freeze. Close your eyes.

Be a hot color. The color feels very warm and hot inside your body. What does the color do to your movement? Be that hot color in movement. Freeze. Be a cool color. Move as this cool color.

Feedback Session

How do you feel? What happened when you were moving without words or sounds? How was your energy different when you added sounds to your movement?

Group Improvisation

You're at a funeral. Pick one color. It can be your favorite color, your least favorite color, a hot color or a cool color. Let the color affect your movement. Feel the color inside your body. See what it does to your body rhythm and energy.

Feedback Session

What happened at the funeral? How did the color affect your body? What differences did you notice?

Divide Into Groups Of Three Or Four

Each group will create an improvisation. Each person should have an objective, action and obstacle. (See Appendix J for definitions of objectives, actions and obstacles.) You can choose to be your favorite color, your least favorite color, a hot color or a cool color. Your improvisation can be verbal or non-verbal. Some people in the improv may talk. Others may be silent. That's up to you. You'll have twenty-five minutes to rehearse and then you'll present your improvisations to the group.

Feedback Session

Let's guess what each person's color was. What did you notice about each person in terms of movement? How did you know they were a certain type of color?

Assignment

Take thirty minutes this week and go out in public and be one color. See how it affects your interactions with other people. Go to a neighborhood where you don't live so you won't run into people you know. Take notes in your journal and we'll share our experiences in the next class.

It was a beautiful moment when I discovered that it is when I don't think
then I am most responsive to others, most aware of what goes on around me, and function best.

— Krishnamurti, Spiritual teacher

Here And Now Exercise
15-30 minutes

PURPOSE: Enhances spontaneity
Improves ability to live in the moment

Procedure

Let's make a big circle. Close your eyes. What are you feeling right now? Open your eyes and we will go around the circle. Each person will say a word or do a gesture expressing what he or she is feeling right at THIS MOMENT. You may do a gesture, sound or a movement. We'll go around the circle ten times. Each time you may have a different gesture, sound or movement.

Feedback Session

What did it feel like? Did you catch yourself thinking? When did it work best for you?

Variations

Let's do the same exercise, but I'll ask you different questions as we go around the circle. Remember to close your eyes and get an image as I ask each question:

1. What was the highlight of your day yesterday?
2. What drives you crazy?
3. How would you like to be feeling right now?
4. What quality or trait are you trying to bring into your life?

The greater to obstacle, the more the glory in overcoming it.
                                                    — Confucius

Concentration Exercise
30-45 minutes

PURPOSE: Develops concentration skills
Develops listening skills
Builds memory skills

Notes to the Leader

Present this exercise as if it is extremely easy to do. It isn't easy, but your group will find it easier to do, if you tell them it's easy to do.

Procedure

I'd like three volunteers to come up to the front of the room. I'll give you each a letter. You are A, you are B, and you are C. I'd like A and C to each pick a topic to talk about. You should be excited about your topic. Each of you is going to discuss separate topics with B, who is standing in the center between A and C. B must carry on a conversation with A and C at the **same** time. B shouldn't just respond with "Yes, that's interesting, that's nice." He must have a **real** conversation with each person. A and C should pick entirely different topics to discuss with B. A and C talk to B at the same time.

Variation 1

This is a more complicated way to do the exercise. A and C, halfway through the exercise, can pick up each other's topics. A will talk about C's topic. C will talk about A's topic. A and C must be listening to each other, as well as having a conversation with B. B goes along with it and continues the conversation with A and C. A and C must be able to **hear** what the other person is saying.

Variation 2

I'd like four people to go to the front of the room. You're all different letters — A, B, C and D. A and B will face each other. C and D will face each other. Each couple will stand about three feet apart. I'll give each couple a subject to talk about. You MUST stick to that one subject. In about three minutes, I'd like couple A-B to talk about what couple C-D is talking about. And couple C-D will talk about what couple A-B is talking about. That means that you both must listen to what your partner is saying as well as listen to what the other couple is saying. You'll have all of your antennae out listening.

Variation 3

I'd like four people to come to the front of the room. You are two couples and you are doing two totally different improvisations at the same time. After two minutes, couple A-B must listen to couple C-D's improv and C-D must listen to A-B's improv. I'll tell each couple, secretly, who they are and where they are. For example: Couple A-B is a travel agent and customer and couple C-D is a husband and wife having a disagreement. I'll give the cue when to switch and continue with the other couple's improvisation.

Feedback Session

What was the experience like for you? What did those of you watching notice? Could you do two things at the same time? How easy is it to do two things at the same time? Did it get easier as the exercise went on?

The body is a sacred garment.
— Martha Graham

Movement Qualities
45-90 minutes

PURPOSE: Enhances movement vocabulary
Heightens awareness of your body and how you move
Encourages play

Notes to the Leader

Remind your group to be gentle with their bodies. Everyone will become excited as they move their bodies in new ways. You want them to be careful that they don't strain or hurt themselves.

You may choose to start the movement exercise with everyone's eyes closed. When they can't see anyone else, they're less self-conscious.

Procedure

Everyone should spread out in the room. Find your own space. Make sure you have room to swing your arms, so you won't hit anyone else. I'll say one word and you'll move your body to that word. You are not relating to anyone else in this exercise. You are in your own space. This exercise is non-verbal. You are just moving your body and not making any sounds.

Movement

Twisting: Start moving your body gently with twisting motions. Twist your hands, your hips, your head and shoulders. Move through space twisting. Don't relate to anyone else in the room as we do these movement qualities. Just feel your whole body twisting. You can twist one body part. Find the subtleties. You can twist with your whole body.

Wringing: Let your whole body wring, your hips and legs, and your torso. Feel your whole body wringing. Move through space, slowly wringing your way through space.

Flowing: Let your body flow through space. Feel its gentleness and ease. Be aware of each body part as you flow like a stream.

Slapping: Start with only one body part. Slap with that part. Then add another part of our body slapping. Move through space slapping the space.

Flipping: Have your body do flipping motions. Stay in one place. See how many individual body parts can flip. It may be a big flip or a small flip. Now move through space flipping.

Vibrating: Let your body vibrate. You might want to start with one body part vibrating and then add other parts. Vibrate through space. Don't relate to anyone else.

Shimmering: Let your body shimmer. Your whole body shimmers. What does it feel like? What kind of people shimmer? Move through space shimmering.

Bending: Have your body bend. How many different ways can it bend? Do small bending movements and large bending movements. Let your body bend through space.

Unfolding: Let one body part unfold. Let another body part unfold. What image do you have for unfolding? Let another body part unfold. Let your whole body unfold like a flower in space. Now start moving around the room unfolding.

Swaying: Let your body gently sway. Move through space swaying. What kind of person sways?

Exploding: Stand still. Let one body part explode. Let another body part explode. Slowly let other parts explode and then let your body explode through space. Be careful not to bump into anyone else. Don't relate to anyone else. Explode through space.

Collapsing: Let your body collapse. How does it collapse? What collapses first? Collapse through space. What do you notice?

Stretching: Stretch one body part. Stretch another body part. Explore how each body part stretches. Stretch your body through space. What kind of character stretches through space?

Notes to the Leader

As you're leading this movement exercise, encourage people to exaggerate the movement. Example: To exaggerate the swaying movement, you can suggest they move as if they were all being blown by hurricane winds.

Or you can ask them to bring the movement inside their bodies and do the movement in a small way. On a scale of one to ten, the movement is now a one or two. They'll take the essence of the movement and put it inside their body. Example: A swaying movement might look like a tiny candle as they move their head. You can give them metaphors as they exaggerate the movement or make the movement smaller. An image often helps people visualize what they're trying to do with their bodies.

As they move, ask them the following questions:

1. What kind of person moves like this?

2. What does this movement remind you of?

3. What quality does this movement have? Is it light? Is it heavy? Is it bound within your body? Is it staccato? Is the movement sustained?

4. What do you notice about your body when it moves like this?

People can say their answers softly out loud. The answers should be short so as not to disturb the movement. They can answer in a word or two. Example: What kind of character moves like this? You might hear a waiter, a concert conductor and so on.

Notes to the Leader

You take them through the thirteen movement qualities again and they can now use their voices and find out what each sound feels like with their *body* and *voice*.

Feedback Session

What did you notice in doing the movement? What did you notice using your voice? What qualities felt comfortable for you? What qualities felt uncomfortable?

Notes to the Leader

Write the different movement qualities on a large sheet of paper so your group can refer to it as they continue with the exercise.

Divide Into Pairs

We're now going to combine the voice and body and do each movement quality again. I'd like you to find a partner and have a conversation. Your body can move or you can remain still and just put the movement quality into your voice. Don't tell your partner what quality you are going to do. Example: One person does Shimmering and his partner does Slapping. It helps to feel the movement inside your body first, and then let it come out through your voice. You can have a conversation about anything you'd like to talk about.

Group Improvisation

Let's all make a circle. One person starts a story. Each person adds one line. When you add a line, you must be using one of the movement qualities with your body and voice.

Group Improvisation

Pick one of the movement qualities: wringing, twisting, flowing, slapping, flipping vibrating, shimmering, bending, unfolding, swaying, exploding or stretching.

Each person is an expert on a special animal. This animal can be a real one or a fantasy animal i.e. a wollytangeroo. I will appoint an MC. The MC will introduce you and ask you your name and about your specific animal, its habits and so on. Each of you will talk for about forty seconds. The rest of you who are listening should remain in character.

Notes to the Leader

You can stop the improv at any point, and say "Freeze." You can ask them to make their movements and sounds small, perhaps on a scale of 1-10, their movements are a 2 or 3. Or you can ask them to make their voice and movements large, an 8 or 9.

Group Improvisation

We will do another animal improvisation. Close your eyes. This time picture the exact OPPOSITE movement quality to the one you just did. Example: If you did exploding, you might do collapsing. You are at an animal convention and you're meeting several people in the room to talk about your animal. Even when you're listening, keep the quality in your body and gestures. Make sure your voice and body manifest and personify that one movement quality.

Feedback Session

What did you notice? What did you see other people doing? What were your interactions like? What did you notice about your body and how you moved differently? What did you learn from this exercise? What did you notice about your voice in terms of rate, pitch, volume, rhythm, intonation, clipping vowels or elongating vowels?

Variation

I'm going to set up 2-person improvisations. Each person should pick one quality to be. After each improvisation, the group will guess what quality you chose.

The truth of someone is in his spontaneous responses, not the edited ones.
— William Esper, acting teacher

Box Closing In
15-30 minutes

PURPOSE: Inspires imagination and creativity
Increases ability to live in the moment

Notes to the Leader

Skills in mime are not important for this exercise.

Procedure

Find your own space in the room. Make sure you have enough space around you. Don't face anyone else. Close your eyes. Feel a box around you. It can be made of any material- wood, gold, chiffon, whatever material you choose. Feel the box around you. You are inside the box.

Movement

Open your eyes. Feel the sides of your box with your hands. Go around the inside of your box. Feel every corner, nook and cranny of the box.

Your box becomes smaller and smaller. Let this happen slowly. Then let your box get bigger and bigger so you can fit five people inside your box with you. Now let your box go back to its original size when you first visualized it.

Try to find a way out of your box. Find a reason why you must get out of your box. Do this slowly. You can take up to five minutes to get out of your box. Find a way out and emerge from your box.

Feedback Session

How did it feel? Could you visualize your box? Could you see it becoming larger and then smaller? How did you find a way out of your box?

Variation 1

Do the same exercise, but this time an animal is in the box with you. Visualize what animal is with you in your box. It might be an elephant, or even a mouse.

Variation 2

Everyone will have a partner. You'll be in the same box. You can talk or remain silent, but you must find a way out of your box once you have created the box together. Notice how connected you are to the person in the box with you.

Notes to the Leader

For Variation 2, you might want to do the exercise with the people in the box talking. Then have the partners do it silently. What differences do they notice when they talk or remain silent?

Above all, you must remain open and fresh and alive to any new idea.
— Sir Laurence Olivier, actor

Object by the Bed Exercise
30-60 minutes

PURPOSE: Increases self-awareness
Enhances spontaneity

Notes to the Leader

At one of your meetings, ask members to put an object next to their bed for one week. It shouldn't be food or a live animal. It can be a memento, a book, or anything else that will fit next to their bed. They should see it at least once or twice a day.

Procedure

Find your own space in the room and close your eyes. Remember the object that you put by your bed. See it, feel it, taste it, smell it, touch it. See it in all of its details.

Movement

Slowly start to transform and become your object. Move as your object would move, if it could move. Don't relate to anyone else. Pick one or two qualities of your object. What qualities are you most aware of? Transform slowly to a person, and put the essence of these qualities in your body.

Group Improvisation

This improvisation is done in silence. You are in a bank line waiting to cash a check. Be the essence of your object while you wait in the line. Freeze.

Movement

Pick an object that is the opposite of the one that was by your bed. It should be opposite in terms of weight, size, color and texture. See this object in your mind and feel it inside your body. Let your body transform to this object.

Group Improvisation

You're at a car race. You're watching the race. Be the essence of the object that is opposite to the one you placed by your bed. You may add your voice, if you like.

Feedback Session

Was this easy or difficult for you? What parts of the exercise were the easiest for you? What parts or the exercise were challenging? Let's go around and say what object you placed by your bed. Share the qualities your object had. Say the object you picked that was the opposite of the one by your bed. What were the qualities of that object? How did you personify it in your body?

Variation 1

We'll do the same exercise next week. This time bring in an object from home that you would like to 'become.'

Judgment kills creativity.
— Anonymous

Float Your Judges Away
30-60 minutes

PURPOSE: To get rid of our judges

Notes to the Leader

This exercise is life-changing. We all have judges that stop and inhibit us from being our most creative and wonderful selves.

It is important to do the *Relaxation Series* (p. 71), or parts of it, before this exercise. Make sure as you provide the guided imagery that you allow enough time for each part that you say. Take your time. Have a box of tissues available in case people cry.

Procedure

How do we get rid of our judges, who stop us from being all we can be and doing all we can do in our lives?

Lie down or sit in a chair, whichever is more comfortable for you. Close your eyes. Relax your body. Let your body sink into the earth.

Remember a situation where you felt judged. Relive that situation.

See a person who judges you. See his or her face. What do they look like? See the textures, colors, faces and everything in as much detail as you can. What were the words spoken or unspoken? Hear what was said and see what happened. Take a minute or two to relive your experience of being judged.

Find a way to float this person or people away. You can float him away on a piece of chiffon or however you'd like to do it. See him disappear. Bring it to a close. Come back to this space, this room. Feel your body underneath you. Feel the earth. Move your hands and toes. Come back into your body. Rub your hands together. Touch your face. Slowly sit up and roll up to a standing position.

Feedback

Find a partner. Share any part of this exercise that you wish. If you don't want to share anything, that's fine, too. You each will have five minutes to share whatever you wish.

Come back together as a group. What was this like for you? How did it feel?

What did it feel like to float your judges away? Be gentle with yourself. This technique is invaluable and the more you use it, the easier it will be to float them away.

Notes to the Leader

Let anyone share when you are together in the group. This is a very powerful exercise and it is important to let whoever wants to share their experience do so. Often you will find that a person's judge is himself or herself. People are hard on themselves and when we release that judge, we feel freer. Letting go of the judges brings peace.

Assignment

Use this technique whenever you sense you are being judged. I have found in my own life, that the more I do this exercise, the faster and easier the judges disappear.

Notes to the Leader

I tell the group that I've done this exercise for thirty years and most of the time I float away my judges in a matter of seconds. Practicing this technique is important and it will get easier each time you do it.

I hope that the trip would be the best of all journeys: a journey into ourselves.

— Shirley MacLaine, actress

Perfect People Party *
90-120 minutes

PURPOSE: Encourages risk taking
Develops empathy for other people
Increases observational skill

Notes to the Leader

In order to create a safe environment, this exercise is only to be performed with a group that has been together for several sessions and is very comfortable working together. During the exercise there will be no violence, no smoking and no drinking.

This exercise should be done outside of class, if possible. The party can be held on a Sunday evening from 6-8 p.m. I found that most people are available Sunday evenings. When I taught a 10-week session, I gave one party per session. Most of my students had taken classes for a year or more, so attended several Perfect People Parties. The parties get richer and richer for those people. The first party is always a bit scary and people tend to play it safe. By the second or third party, people take greater risks.

I usually hold the party at someone's house or a location close to where the sessions are held.

Assign this exercise at your first or second meeting so your group has at least five or six weeks to prepare for the party. The party is held about two-thirds of the way through the session.

Procedure

Please take these notes on this assignment.

1. I would like all of you to pick a type of person to be at a party we'll have in six weeks. It is called a *Perfect People Party.*
2. Start working on this assignment this week. Don't wait until the fifth week.
3. You'll come to the party as a specific type of person – a bag lady, a priest, a belly dancer, a truck driver and so on. Pick someone whom you would really like to be. This person should not be a famous person.

4. Begin to follow people and get ideas for the type of person you'd like to be.
5. After you pick your person, write an autobiography of this person in your journal. Write down the similarities and differences between you and this person. Do this in PENCIL, because as you research this person, you might find more similarities or differences than you originally thought.
6. Make other notes in your journal. Write stream of consciousness, which means just letting your thoughts flow. Write as this person would write.
7. Men can be women. Women can be men. You can be any age you choose.
8. Don't tell anyone in the group whom you're coming as to the party. It will be a surprise for everyone.
9. I'll be participating in this exercise and coming as a certain type of person. I won't be the teacher.
10. Find a costume or clothes to wear.
11. Bring food to the party that this person would likely bring to a party, if they would bring food.
12. There is no smoking or drinking of alcohol. If your character does smoke or drink, you must find a reason why he/she can't do so at the party.
13. Find the reason why you are coming to this place, wherever we are having the party. Each person will have his own reason for coming to the party.
14. I'd like you to be this person in public for at least an hour or more during the next few weeks. There was a man in his fifties who came to the party as a Nun. He went out in public dressed as a Nun and everyone believed he was a Nun. When you go out in public as your person, you will strengthen your own belief that you really can be this person. It'll be exciting to have interactions with various people as your character. I suggest you go to a different neighborhood than the one where you live, so no one will recognize you.
15. Fix a meal at your home as this person.
16. The improvisation will last for one and a half hours. Stay in character. You may find there are some people that you may not want to talk to as much as others. That's fine.
17. Pick a character who you would like to be. Whose skin would it be fun to live in for an hour and a half?
18. I will blink the lights at the end of the time and then we'll take thirty minutes to process and ground the exercise.
19. There will be no violence at the party.
20. Your transformation will begin the morning of the party. Your character will be with you during the day. As you start to get ready for the party, you'll start transforming to your character.
21. Have fun with this exercise.

Notes to the Leader

When you blink the lights at the end of the party, say to your group, "Close your eyes. Let your body relax. Feel your feet on the floor. Feel your hands rubbing together. Feel your breath. Feel your face. Slowly come back to this reality. When I turn the lights on, we'll all sit down."

It's important to bring them back to reality slowly. Let them sense their bodies in the room before you talk about the exercise. Let your group know that you'll be available after the feedback session if they still don't feel grounded. If people see you for more grounding, do some physical exercises with them, i.e. jumping jacks, yelling, pounding the floor and so on. Acting silly and doing physical exercises help bring them back to reality.

Feedback Session

What was the party like for you? How did you research your character? What happened when you went out in public as your character? How did people react to you? Let's go around the room and say what type of character you were.

Assignment

Answer the following questions in your journal:

1. What sub-personality were you at the party? Realize that who you were at the party are different parts of yourself. What worked well for you?
2. What needed more research and grounding?
3. What kind of interactions did you have?
4. What would you have done differently in your preparation?

It is important to write in your journals either this evening or tomorrow. This is part of the grounding process. You'll learn a lot by writing these notes. We'll discuss more about this exercise in the next session.

Notes to the Leader

Discuss other things that came up for people at the *Perfect People Party*. Your participants will have a chance to reflect on their experience and might have other questions, ideas and feedback. At the next session, ask your group what else they would like to share about their experiences at the *Perfect People Party*.

* This exercise was adapted from an exercise in **A Book on the Open Theater** by Robert Pasoli. Our *Perfect People Parties* are different from what Robert Pasoli wrote, but I got the idea of the *Perfect People Party* from his wonderful book.

We are what we think.
— Buddha

The Most Exciting Things
15-30 minutes

PURPOSE: To increase vulnerability
To have participants get to know each other better
To increase connection in your group
To be spontaneous

Procedure

Make a large circle. This exercise is not about thinking. It's about saying the first thing that comes into your mind. It's about spontaneity. I'd like you share the most exciting things that have happened in your life. It can be a phrase or a sentence. We'll go around the circle seven times.

Find a partner. Do this exercise again. Listen carefully to your partner as we go back and forth with exciting things that have happened in our lives. You may end up remembering things that you haven't thought about in years.

Feedback Session

What was this like for you? How did you feel inside your body? What was it like getting to know your partner? What was it like for your partner to get to know you in this way?

Every child is an artist. The problem is how to remain an artist once he grows up.
— Pablo Picasso

Closing Exercise
30-45 minutes

PURPOSE: Enhances what each participant received from the group
Gives closure to the group experience

TOOLS: Drawing board-foam core
Large sheet of newsprint, 18" x 24"
Crayons or markers

Procedure

Each of you should have a drawing board, sheet of paper and drawing tools in front of you. Sit up straight and close your eyes. Draw with your non-dominant hand. If you are right handed, draw with your left hand. If you are left handed, draw with your right hand. Trust the first image you get. What did you receive during the group/retreat/weekend/today?

Notes to the Leader

You, too, can draw what you received. The fact that you're drawing and sharing will mean a lot to your group, especially in the feedback session.

As you sense the drawings are being finished, you say to your group, "Write any notes you like on the back of your drawing or in your journals as you finish the drawing." The reason you say this after their drawings are almost completed, is that if you say it too early on, they might not draw, but instead begin writing. This last drawing will be something they can take away and treasure.

Feedback Session

Let's share our drawings. Show your drawing and say anything you'd like to know about it.

Notes to the Leader

One person's drawing can trigger what another person also received from the group. Sharing their drawings at this point is a way to ground the learning and is a gift for you and each person in your group. It tells you what each person gained from the group. It clarifies, for each person, what they learned and the insights they are taking away from the group.

Variation

Have your group stand in a circle. Ask them to close their eyes. You say, "What is one thing you will be taking away from this group? What is one thing you learned?" They open their eyes and you go around the circle and they share in a sentence of two what they are taking away from the group. Saying it out loud grounds it and it's wonderful to hear what everyone says.

Intermediate Exercises

For by now you know that I have spent many hours seeking the wisdom of nature—
for it is always in the immediate presence of the Creator.

— Winston Abbott, writer

Elements: Earth-Air-Fire-Water
60-90 minutes

PURPOSE: Increases movement vocabulary
Explores relationship to the natural environment
Heightens appreciation of rhythms

Notes to the Leader

It's ideal if the movement in this exercise can be done outdoors. The space can be a big lawn or open area. Spring, summer and fall are the best seasons for the exercise. Being outdoors lets students feel the elements around their bodies as they are doing each element. A country setting is ideal.

If you don't have an outdoor space available, a large room is fine. You can play a tape with nature effects if you feel it would help create the mood. Or you can leave it up to each person's imagination to create the mood.

There are many parts to this exercise. If you chose to do all the parts, it could take several hours. You can pick one section that will fit into the time frame that you have available.

Procedure

Let's all sit in a large circle. We'll go around the circle and each person says his impression of what element each person is: air, fire, earth or water.

It's interesting to see how the group views you. There may be different opinions as to what element each person is. Or, we might find that there is a consensus of opinion on what element each person is. Certain people might be a combination of two or more elements. Try and focus on what element stands out. There is no right or wrong in this work.

Movement

Earth: Lie down and close your eyes. Get an image of the earth. How does it feel? What do you notice? What is your rhythm? Open your eyes and stand up and move as earth. During these movement exercises, you're not relating to anyone else in the group. Please be respectful of each other's space as you move.

Water: Lie down and close your eyes. Get an image of water. Put water around you. Put water inside you. You are water. What's your rhythm? Open your eyes and move as water. You can use different levels in movement. You can remain lying down, or go on your knees or stand up. You are water. You are moving through water. Know that you can easily breathe in water.

Air: Lie down and close your eyes. Get an image of air. Let it move through you and around you. What does your body weight feel like? There is air inside you and around you. What is your rhythm?

Fire: Lie down and close your eyes, or you can remain standing. Get an image of fire. How do you feel? What's your center? Where is your center? Open your eyes and move around as fire. What is your rhythm?

Divide Into Pairs

Pick one element you would like to be: air, fire, water, or earth. Don't tell your partner what element you've chosen. Move non-verbally as that element. Always connect to your partner in some way, either by touching or looking at each other. Freeze. Keep the element going on, even when you freeze. Come back to neutral.

Keep the same partner. Pick another element you would like to be. Don't tell your partner what element you've chosen. Move to that element. You may add sound to your movement this time. Always connect with your partner in some way.

Group Improvisation

Close your eyes. Pick one element you'd like to become. Feel it with your whole body. Pick the element that was most difficult for you. Open your eyes. You are in a line at a movie theater, waiting to purchase a ticket. See how that element affects your body and voice.

Feedback Session

What did each element feel like? What elements were most comfortable for you? What elements were most difficult or challenging?

Vocal Part Of The Exercise

Lie down. Close your eyes. Go with the first image you receive. Breathe. Relax your jaw, tongue and lips. You're now going to make sounds matching each of the elements- earth, air, fire and water. Let the sound of that element move through you.

Begin with EARTH sounds. Where do they begin? What part of your body are you most in touch with when you make earth sounds? Make sure your throat and jaw are relaxed.

Make AIR sounds. What do you now notice about your voice? What do you notice about the way you breathe? Relax.

Make FIRE sounds. Make sure your throat is open. You don't have to yell. See where the sounds begin when you make a fire sound. What does it feel like? How is the fire sound different than the earth sound? How is it different than the air sound? Relax.

Make WATER sounds. What vowels are most pronounced in making water sounds?

Movement

Spread out in the room.

Earth: Make earth sounds and earth movement. Tie the two together. How does it feel to be earth with your body and voice? How is your body connected to your voice? Relax.

Air: Move as air and make air sounds. Where is your center of gravity? What do you notice about your body and voice? Relax.

Fire: Make fire sounds and move as fire. You might want to start with one body part and then add different body parts as you move as fire. Make sure your voice stays relaxed and doesn't get tense. Relax.

Water: Let your voice become water along with your body. How do you flow? What is your rhythm? What does your body feel like? What is your center of gravity?

Notes to the Leader

Be aware that each person interprets the elements differently. One person may make earth sounds with a gentle low voice. His movements may be slow and deliberate while another person may find tremendous power in his voice and yell, while his body steam rolls through space.

One person may interpret fire as a tranquil still flame and may choose to make a quiet sound and not move at all. Another person may see fire as wild and make loud and erratic sounds as he dashes through space. Allow your group to have their own interpretations, and support all of their choices.

Group Improvisation

You're at a nightclub. You'll be meeting other people. Pick one of the qualities (earth, air, fire or water) and let your body exaggerate that movement. Let your voice also exaggerate the sounds it makes. Freeze.

Now pick another quality (earth, air, fire or water) and exaggerate that quality with your voice and body. Keep relating to the people in the nightclub. See what happens. Freeze.

You're still in the nightclub. Pick one more quality and exaggerate that quality with your voice and body. Freeze.

You are in a hotel lobby. Pick one quality (earth, air, fire or water) and underplay it. From one to ten, you're a one or two. See how this affects how you move. You may feel this quality more internally than externally.

Pick another quality (earth, air, fire or water). Let it be understated. It can be a one or two on the scale from one to ten. How does your body feel now? Are you feeling the quality inside your body? Freeze. Relax.

Feedback Session

How did that feel? What did you notice?

Procedure

Spread out in the room. Close your eyes. Pick just one element you would like to explore (earth, air, fire or water). Create an autobiography for this character. (See Suggestions for Autobiographical Questions for Characters, Appendix E.)

Two-Person Improvisation

I'll tell each couple who you are, where you are, what your objective is and what element I would like you to be. When the improvisation is finished, we'll guess what element you each were. I might ask you to exaggerate the element or keep it very small within your body and voice.

Three- or Four-Person Improvisation

Each group will have forty minutes to rehearse a scene. The scene should have the following:
1. Who you are
2. A place: where you are
3. An objective: each person has an objective

4. An element for each person: earth, air, fire or water
5. As we watch each scene, we'll guess what element each person is. You can exaggerate the element or keep it very small. You can go anywhere between one and ten on how big or small you make the element.

Group Improvisation

You are men and women in your 30's, 40's or 50's. You have one or two aging parents. I'll ask one person to be the group therapist. Each person should pick one element they'd like to be and keep that one element throughout the improvisation. The session is about how to help our aging parents.

Feedback Session

What did you notice about becoming the element? What parts of the exercise were most enjoyable for you? What parts were challenging for you?

Let's define what qualities each element has. We'll make a list of each element and its qualities.

Notes to the Leader

Here are some qualities that people have suggested for the list:

Air: floating, light, in the clouds, vaporous, unattached, fluffy, not direct, unfocused, weightless, philosophical, receptive

Water: flowing, passive, rhythmic, irresponsible, indirect, expansive, connectedness, calming, slow

Earth: solid, centered, secure, dependable, receptive, open, clear, well-defined, rational, rooted, growing, calm

Fire: burning, unpredictable, direct, intense, dramatic, spontaneous, impulsive, strong, abrupt, dominating, powerful

Assignments

1. Notice in your everyday life what elements people are. What elements are your family members, your best friends and people you work with? What elements are you attracted to? What elements would you like to bring into your life?
2. Try and be each element in public this week. Be that element for twenty minutes. You might be doing your errands or taking a walk. What do you notice happening in your voice and body as you take on each element? Make some notes on these experiences in your journal.

3. Get together with someone from the group and cook a meal being one of the elements. How does each element affect your voice and body? Discuss how you felt after your meal.

4. Follow one person for twenty minutes and start to 'become' this person. What element do they personify? Pick a person who would be challenging for you to become. Bring that person into the group next week. In the next session, I'll set up an improvisation and introduce each person to the group. Find someone whom you would really like to be. Have fun.

In the beginner's mind, there are many possibilities. In the expert's mind there are few.
— Shunryu Suzuki, Zen priest and writer

Musical Tune
30-45 minutes

PURPOSE: To increase your movement vocabulary
To take risks

Procedure

Find a space in the room. Close your eyes. Think of a musical tune that you like. Let the musical tune go through your body. Feel it in every pore and vein.

What is the feeling of this tune? Is it happy? Is it sad? Is it melancholy? Is it upbeat? What does this musical tune feel like in your body?

Open your eyes and move around with the essence of this musical tune in your body. You aren't singing the tune. It's INSIDE of you and influences how you move your body, and how you go through space.

You can blow it up so it is way over the top. You can tone it down, so the tune is very soft in your body. Play around with all of the variations of how this tune feels in your body. Let the tune be in just one body part. Let the tune spread to other body parts. Meet other people in the room and be the essence of your musical tune.

Let's do some improvisations. I'll ask two people to volunteer and I'll tell you where you are and who you are. Let the musical tune be the essence of how you move and use your voice. Example: You are in a new car showroom. One of you is the sales person; one of you is the person looking to buy a new car. Keep the essence of your tune in your gestures, movements and voice.

Notes to the Leader

Have your group do the exercise two or three times. Each time, ask them to pick a new musical tune to personify.

Feedback Session

What was this like for you? How did it feel? What did you notice about your movements? What was it like to blow it up big or take it down so the essence was small? What was it like meeting other people?

Could you connect with everyone in the group while keeping your musical tune? Were there some people whose tune and personae didn't jibe with your essence?

Assignment

Do some observations of people you see every day. If they were a musical tune, what tune would they be? What is their rhythm, their beat, and their essence? How do they carry that tune in their body and voice? Do they move slowly? Do they move rapidly? Do they move with lethargy? Do they move with dignity? Are they sprightly? Do they have a lot of energy? How do you feel when you see them move? If you have a conversation with them or know them, how does their energy feel to you, when you're with them? Do people have different musical tunes going on depending on their moods?

Be realistic: Plan for a miracle.
> — Bhagwan Shree Rajneesh,
> Indian mystic and spiritual teacher

Fantasy and Dream
30-60 minutes

PURPOSE: Encourages teamwork
Inspires inner life to come out

TOOLS: One scarf, optional

Notes to the Leader

Always start with a fun and exciting dream or fantasy. The first volunteer shouldn't tell something terrifying or upsetting. The first fantasy should create laughter and fun within your group.

Procedure

Who would like to volunteer to act out a dream or fantasy? I would like to start with a fun and exciting dream or fantasy. I'll give you an example of how this will work. Suppose you fantasize about being a rock star giving a concert at Central Park. You can pick people within the group to act out this fantasy with you. You'll describe all of the characters in your fantasy — your band, dancers, the cheering crowd and so on. People can volunteer for the roles they would like to play. Sometimes, what happens is that what the volunteers choose to play in someone else's fantasy, might indeed, be their own personal fantasy.

You'll explain **exactly** how you would like your fantasy to be and we'll all act it out. You will be in the center, being the rock star that you have always wanted to be.

The same rules apply for enacting a dream. You tell your dream, and then participants will volunteer to be whatever parts of the dream you have described. We can be inanimate things, such as a storm, the wind, lightening, and so on, as well as people and animals. People can volunteer for the roles they would like to play. We will enact the fantasy or dream for as long as the volunteer would like it to be. The volunteer may change different parts of the dream and do side coaching on how a role should be played. He can 'model' how the band drummer might play the drums. We want the dream or fantasy to be as realistic as possible for the group.

The scarf may be used as a blindfold, if the lead person just wants to hear what is going on within his dream or fantasy, rather than seeing it.

Notes to the Leader

There are different ways to enact a dream or fantasy.

1. The person telling the dream can choose to be himself in the dream.

2. He can choose to become another character in the dream.

3. He can choose to stand outside of the dream and watch it unfolding before his eyes. Someone else would be 'him' in the dream.

One exciting element is that the person telling the dream or fantasy may choose to change the ending of the dream. This is wonderful because if someone had an unhappy or scary dream or fantasy, he can change the ending to be a peaceful and happy one.

Feedback Session

What was it like having your fantasy/dream acted out? How did you feel if you were a part of a fantasy/dream? What did you learn? What did you notice when you acted out different parts of a fantasy/dream? Did you have any new insights into yourself? If you were a part of the audience, what did you see?

Nothing is more revealing than movement.

— Martha Graham

Delsarte Exercise
45-60 minutes

PURPOSE: Increases movement vocabulary
Increases emotional flexibility

Notes to the Leader

This exercise can be threatening to people if they're uncomfortable about their sexuality. The pelvis and hips are the sexual centers. This can be the core of many people's tension. Go slowly and gently when you reach the sexual center.

Procedure

A man named François Delsarte developed a theory of movement. I've taken parts of his theory and applied it to this exercise.

The head is the intellectual center. Watch 'heady' or intellectual people. They have most of their energy focused in the head area. 'Head' professions might be professors, mathematicians, and engineers. The chest is the *emotional* center. Highly emotional people often gesture towards their chest and their energy comes from their chest. The pelvis and hips are the *primitive* or *sexual* center. A character like Stanley Kowalski in *A Streetcar Named Desire* functions primarily from his sexual center. We're going to try on each of these centers and see what it does to your movement and your way of relating.

We're first going to work with the *intellectual* center – the head. Spread out in the room. You're standing up. Close your eyes. Imagine that you have a HUGE head. The rest of your body isn't there. It disappears. Feel that you're all HEAD. Open your eyes and move around the space. You have huge eyes, huge ears, a huge brain. Your focus of awareness is in your head.

Group Improvisation

You're in an art museum. You are all head. Feel every tooth in your mouth, eyes blinking, and hairs on your head. Feel your tongue and lips. All of your awareness is in your head. Find one person to talk to. Notice that your voice comes from your head alone. How do you feel? Your breathing comes from your head. The rest of your body has disappeared. You have no other body awareness. Freeze.

Continue the conversation, but be aware of only your FOREHEAD and nothing else. Your voice comes from your forehead. The rest of your body disappears. Freeze. Notice how you use your voice.

Pick someone else to engage in conversation. This time you are all NOSE. The rest of your body disappears. You are one huge nose. See what happens to your voice when you are just a nose. Freeze.

Continue the conversation. Now you are just a MOUTH. Nothing else. The rest of your body disappears. You are a mouth. Freeze.

Mix again with the group. You are all CHIN. Your energy is in your chin. You're waiting in a movie lobby being a chin. Freeze.

Relax. Let your body hang over from your waist and shake your body out.

Feedback Session

What did you notice? What did being each part feel like? What part did you enjoy being the most? What part was difficult to do? How did the movement affect your voice?

Movement

Spread out in the room. We're going to work with the **emotional** center, the chest. Rotate your chest in all directions. Move your chest backwards, forward and side to side. Be gentle. Make your chest puff out. Notice how flexible or inflexible your chest is.

Close your eyes. Imagine that you're all chest. You have an enormous chest. The rest of your body is not there. The rest of your body disappears. Open your eyes and move around. You are CHEST. It can be an extraverted chest.

Group Improvisation

You're at a meeting with your neighbors who live on your block. You must figure out how to clean up the dog poop from the neighborhood. This has been a big problem. Feel that you are all chest as you do this improvisation. Notice how this affects your movement and voice. Freeze.

Feedback Session

What did you notice? How did you act? What was different in having the chest be your emotional center instead of using your head? What were your interactions like? How did the movement affect your voice?

Movement

We're now going to work with the *primitive sexual center*, the hips and pelvis. Rotate your hips in all directions. In order to do this easily, put your feet about six inches apart and pretend to sit i.e. bend your knees. You can now rotate your hips easily. Swing your hips from side to side. Do this gently. Move your hips to the back. Move your hips to the front. Make a circle with your hips. Make a figure-eight with your hips. Write your name gently with your hips. Notice how flexible or inflexible the hips are. It doesn't matter if you can do large or small motions with the hips. Even the slightest movement with your hips gives a message, as you'll soon find out.

Spread out in the room. Close your eyes. Imagine that you are all HIPS and PELVIS. The rest of your body disappears. Open your eyes and move around the room. You're HIPS and PELVIS. You're a hot tamale. What does this feel like? What kind of people move like this?

Group Improvisation

You're in a hotel lobby, either waiting for someone or just hanging out. Decide why you're there. Remember, as you wait, you're all HIPS and PELVIS. You can talk to other people or you may not want to engage in conversation. Notice how you use your voice.

Feedback Session

What did it feel like being all hips and pelvis? What did you notice? What were your interactions like? How was this different than moving from your head or chest centers? How did the movement affect your voice?

Group Improvisation

Close your eyes. You're businessmen and women in a prestigious business firm. You're of equal status. You can pick to be all HEAD or intellectual center, or all CHEST or emotional center, or all HIPS and PELVIS which is your primitive sexual center. You're having a discussion on how to best market or publicize your firm. You want to attract more clients.

Feedback Session

Say to your group, "While we are doing this feedback session, I'd like you to pick one of the areas — head, chest or hips — and be one of those body centers as we process the exercise. Even if you're sitting down, it won't matter. Your energy is coming from whichever center you choose. I'll also pick one of the centers to come from as I conduct the feedback session.

What was the exercise like for you? What did you notice? What was the easiest center for you to do? What was the most difficult center to do? How did each center affect your interactions?

Variation 1

Let's go around the room and each person will say what they think their body center is: head, chest or hips. Each person will then stand up and walk around the room and the group will imitate them. Remember, there's no right or wrong way to do this exercise.

Variation 2

Let's divide into groups of three. I'd like you to structure an improvisation with the following:

1. A place: where you are.

2. An objective: each person has an objective, what you want from the other people.

3. Body center: choose a body center and keep that center throughout the scene, your head, chest or hips.

The improvisation will be done for the group and we'll guess what center you are stressing from your gestures, movement, and voice.

I am always doing that which I cannot do, in order that I may learn how to do it.
— Pablo Picasso

Panel of Experts
45-60 minutes

PURPOSE: Bonds your group
Teaches spontaneity and being in the moment
Highlights spotlighting and listening to each other

Procedure

Three people will be sent out of the room. The group decides what characters the three people will be. Example: They are CEO's of an oil company. The three people enter and the group tells them who they are. The group asks each person on the panel questions and the experts answer the questions to the best of their ability. When you are on the panel and you don't know anything about the subject, pretend you do.

Notes to the Leader

Everyone in your group has a chance to be on the panel of experts. Example: A panel of professors in Early American History, a panel of bearded dragon lizard owners, a panel of snow removal experts. It is important for each panel member to take his role seriously. He is an expert in his chosen area.

Feedback Session

What did you notice? How did it feel? Did you spotlight each other? Were you listening to each other or planning ahead about what you were going to say?

Where the spirit does not work with the hand, there is no art.

— Leonardo Da Vinci

Painting Exercise
45-60 minutes

PURPOSE: Enhances creativity
Develops intuition

TOOLS: Clippings from art magazines of famous paintings
Postcards of paintings you can purchase at an art museum gift shop

Divide Into Pairs

Find a partner. Find someone you haven't worked with or someone you don't know well. Decide who will be A and who will be B. I'm going to give the A's a picture of a painting. The B's will close their eyes. B's eyes are closed throughout the exercise. A's will look at the picture carefully and communicate the essence of the painting to their partner.

The exercise is non-verbal. Through movement and touch, B will get images of what the painting looks like. Example: You can move your partner's arms slowly in circles or set their arms at angles depending on your picture. You can move your partner quickly or slowly. Be respectful of your partner. You don't literally communicate the painting to your partner, i.e. if you have a picture of the Mona Lisa, don't sit your partner down and cross her hands. This exercise may seem abstract, but you will be amazed at how much your partner can pick up by how you're moving their body. You can communicate the essence in terms of shape, color, rhythm, line, composition, mood and textures.

The person who is A will put the essence of the painting in his body, and then begin moving their partner around in different ways to communicate what the painting says.

Then we'll switch positions and B's will communicate a painting to their partner.

Feedback Session

What did you feel like? What did you notice? Could you communicate your painting—the shape, color, rhythm, textures and essence—to your partner?

Movement

Find your own space in the room. Look at your painting again. Move to the essence of your painting. I'll go around, tap you lightly and I'd like you to say what the essence is in one or two words. Feel the essence in your hands, face, shoulders, torso, hips, feet and in your walk.

Group Improvisation

You're in a park. You can talk to other people or remain by yourself. Feel the essence of your painting in your body. You might want to start in silence and then talk to other people. See how the essence of the painting affects your voice.

Feedback Session

What was this like? How did you use your voice and body to communicate the essence of your painting?

Variation

I'll give a picture to one person in the group and that person will try to communicate the painting to the entire group. This person uses his body and voice.

Assignment

Find a picture postcard of a painting you're attracted to and take the postcard home. Move to the essence of the painting. You're free to put on music in the background if you like. Write in your journal about what this experience was like for you.

Life is my college. May I graduate well and earn some honors.

— Louisa May Alcott

Newspaper Article
45-90 minutes

PURPOSE: Increases movement vocabulary
Heightens sensitivity to language
Encourages vulnerability

Notes to the Leader

Bring in twenty newspaper articles that you find interesting. Each article should have a story to tell, a conflict and should be written with a personal point of view. The articles can be funny or sad. The article should have a definite 'feeling' and shouldn't be bland or boring.

You can distribute one article to each person. Another way to do the exercise is to have each person bring in their own article, one that appeals to them.

Procedure

I've brought in many articles. Each person will select one article to read silently. As you read it, begin to have feelings about the words, tone, subject matter and feelings expressed in the article.

Divide Into Pairs

Find a partner. Read your articles to each other. Let the article affect you. Share with your partner what the article means to you. Each one of you will take a turn. Begin to move as the essence of the article. You may choose a word or image to move to. Or you can move to the feeling you had as you read your article. Express the essence of your article in gestures and movement.

Procedure

Come back to the group. Each person will move as the essence of his or her article. I'm going to coach you one at a time. I may ask you to enlarge your movement or to move in ways that will open you up more. Your voice might also be involved.

Notes to the Leader

Coach each person in front of your group for ten to fifteen minutes. Notice ways that you want each person to open up and coach him or her with that objective in mind. What sub-personalities, or parts of each person, would you like to open up more? Example: If a participant is usually serious in your group, you might coach her to be silly and outrageous.

Feedback Session

What did you notice as each person moved? How did it feel? What images stood out for you in the article?

Variation 1

We'll do the same exercise and this time we will use a poem, rather than an article.

Variation 2

We'll do the same exercise. After we move to the feeling of the poem, you'll draw its essence. Use your non-dominant hand. If you are right-handed, use your left hand. If you are left-handed, use your right hand. See page 30 for more about drawing with your opposite hand.

Feedback Session

What did this feel like? Where did you feel the essence of your poem in your body? Did the essence affect your voice? How?

The capacity of inner listening is the basic precondition for creativity. For how else could inspiration come unless you trust it? You listen. You capture an inner impulse. It is completing, or perhaps it is faint and vague. Should you follow it? You let it guide you into territories as yet unknown, you break new ground. You believe in your impulse. You believe yourself.

— Piero Ferrucci, psychologist and writer

Picture Exercise
45-60 minutes

PURPOSE: Enhances imagination
Develops emotional range

Notes to the Leader

Bring in wonderful pictures that appeal to you. They can be from magazines or postcards. These pictures can be of landscapes, people, advertisements and so on. Put the pictures in the center of the room and spread them out.

Procedure

There are pictures in the center of the room. Pick one that appeals to you. Find a place in the room and sit down. Look at the your picture. You're going to create a character based on your picture. What feeling does your picture evoke inside of you?

Movement

Find your own space. Slowly transform to a character based on your picture. You're alone in a room of your house or apartment. You're doing a task. What task would you be doing if you were alone? What does your room look like? You may talk aloud to yourself, if your character would talk aloud when she is alone.

Decide to change your clothes. You might be getting ready to go to a party or event. Put the clothes on that you would like wear. This is done in pantomime.

Group Improvisation

You are in a park. Be your character. You may talk to one other person or remain quiet. Have an objective. Freeze. Close your eyes.

Get an image of a character OPPOSITE from the person you just portrayed. Trust your first image. You're in the park. You may talk to other people or remain quiet. Freeze. Relax.

Feedback Session

What did you notice? How did you feel? Each person will share their picture with the group. Tell what inspired you in creating your character. Tell which qualities in your picture that you picked to become.

Tell the group about the opposite character you became and which qualities you chose to personify.

Variation 1

Each person brings in their favorite picture and bases a character upon that picture.

Variation 2

Next week we're going to do a group improvisation. Pick a favorite picture that you love. Base a character on it. You'll work on this at home. Create an autobiography and write it in your journal. (See Appendix E: Autobiographical Questions for Characters.) Decide how you want to dress. Go out in public as this person before you come to class next week. When you enter the room next week, you'll be this person. You'll be people who are taking a class together, but your 'character' will be the person in your picture.

Variation 3

Find a picture that you love. Work for thirty minutes at home with your picture. Create a two-minute improvisation based on the essence of this picture. You can present it for the group in abstract movement, or you can create an improvisation where you are talking to us. You can do whatever you wish with those two minutes. Your presentation is based on the essence of your picture. On your own, try different things. Experiment and see what you'd like to share.

My heart leaps up
when I behold
A rainbow in the sky:
So was it when my
life began;
So is it now I am a man;
So be it when I shall
grow old,
Or let me die!
The child is
father of the man;
And I could wish
my days to be
Bound each to each
by natural piety.

— William Wordsworth

Poems
30-60 minutes

PURPOSE: Encourages inner life to come out
Heightens sensitivity to language

Notes to the Leader

Find at least twenty poems that you love. They should have rich and wonderful images in them. Type each poem on a separate piece of paper.

Procedure

I've brought in many poems and I'm going to give you each one poem to look over. First, read it silently and then, aloud. Pick one or two lines that appeal to you and memorize them.

Movement

Take the one or two lines that you've memorized and do these lines in movement. You can act out the lines or move to the essence of the lines. Be respectful of each other's space.

Notes to the Leader

After the group has moved for three minutes say, "Freeze." Divide the group in half so each group can watch the other half move.

Group Improvisation

Find your own space in the room. Create an autobiography based on the one or two lines that you memorized. You're in an airport. You can be waiting for someone to arrive or waiting to take a flight. Find a voice for your character. Freeze. Blow it up and exaggerate what you're doing. Freeze. Now make your movements and voice very small. Put the essence of the poem inside your body.

Feedback Session

How did you feel? Everyone now reads his poem aloud. What images from your poem did you choose when you developed your character?

Nothing so clearly and inevitably reveals the inner man than movement and gesture.
It is quite possible, if one chooses, to conceal and dissimulate behind words or paintings . . .
but the moment you move, you stand revealed, for good or ill, for what you are.
— Doris Humphrey, dancer and choreographer

Shape Exercise
60-90 minutes

PURPOSE: Promotes sensitivity to nature
Encourages ability to emphasize

TOOLS: Paper
Drawing utensils
Drawing board

Notes to the Leader

This exercise is best done in nature, such as in a park, or in the woods. The place should be quiet so your group can be alone and explore nature. The ideal place would be a lovely place in the woods.

Procedure

We'll be going on a long walk in the woods. This exercise in non-verbal. As soon as we leave this room, we're silent until we return to this room. I'll be giving different directions when we're in the woods, quietly and briefly. Be respectful of each other's space. You'll have plenty of room to move around.

Movement

In the woods: Become one with the objects around you.

Opening: Find something that's opening. Become it. Become a piece of nature in movement. Watch it as you do your movement. Move away from it and do the opening movement.

Growing: Find something in the woods that is growing. Become it. Grow with the object. Imitate it as you watch it grow.

Unfolding: Find something close to you that is unfolding, such as a leaf or a piece of bark. Become one with it. Unfold with it.

Closing: Find something that is closing, such as a flower or a leaf. Try and imitate it as you watch it. Feel yourself closing. What does it feel like?

Shrinking: Find something in the woods that is shrinking. Become one with it and feel one part of your body shrinking. Then feel your whole body shrinking.

Folding: Find something that's folding. Try to do a folding movement with your whole body or one body part.

Let's walk back to our room. On the way back, blow up and exaggerate one element that you want to be: opening, growing, unfolding, closing, shrinking or folding. The exercise is non-verbal.

Symbolic Drawing

We're back in the room. Draw the most powerful image you saw or felt in the woods. You may draw it and then write about it. Use your non-dominant hand when you draw. See page 30 for more about drawing with your opposite hand.

Feedback Session

Let's share our drawings. Say something about your drawing and about your experience in the woods.

Movement

Put your drawing in front of you. Get an image either from your drawing or from the walk. Feel that image in your body. Create an autobiography of a person. Move as that person. Be respectful of each other's space as you move.

Divide Into Pairs

Create an improvisation with the following things:

1. Who are you? What is your relationship to the other person?

2. Where are you? What is the place of your scene?

3. What is your objective and action? Have an objective, i.e. what you want from the other person and an action: a verb with how you are going to get what you want from the other person. (See Appendix J: Glossary of Terms, page 227.)

During your improvisation, keep the essence of your nature image with you. You'll have twenty minutes to practice.

Presentation

Each couple will do their improvisation for the group. The group will guess what part of nature they were- shrinking, flowing, opening, and so on.

Feedback Session

What qualities did you most enjoy moving to? Were there any movement qualities that were challenging for you?

Variation 1

We'll do the whole exercise and we will remain in the woods for the improvisation part.

Variation 2

Vocal sounds can be added when you move. What kind of sound would UNFOLDING make? Make sure that you keep your throat open and your jaw relaxed as you make the different sounds for each element.

We must expand our perceptions of ourselves.

— Uta Hagen, actress and acting teacher

Stereotypes
45-60 minutes

PURPOSE: Inspires compassion for people unlike yourself
Enhances ability to pick up non-verbal behavior

Notes to the Leader

Be sensitive as you work with your group. The stereotypes you work with may overlap the lives of some people in your group.

Procedure

Let's make a list of stereotypical characters. I'll write them down on a large sheet of paper. **Remember, this exercise is not about making fun of anyone.** In this exercise, we will explore how stereotypes are created and hopefully, develop a compassionate understanding of them. A stereotype reflects ideas, both positive and negative, that people have about others who are different from themselves. While there may an element of truth in a stereotype, we must be sensitive in our portrayals of stereotypical characters.

We'll pick one to work with as a group. Example: Jewish mother. What is the stereotype of a Jewish mother? I'll write down your answers. Examples: Feeds you, high voice, kvetch, lays guilt, controlling, picky, cooks all of the time, smothering, loving, wants you to have clean clothes, wants you to be successful, and so on. For every seemingly 'negative characteristic' you might want to find its opposite in a positive trait.

Group Improvisation

We'll do an improvisation where you are all Jewish mothers, to the hilt. Men can be women. Let's exaggerate it. Each person will portray almost a caricature of the stereotypical Jewish mother. We are all at a board meeting of the Humane Society. We are all board members, discussing our fall fund-raiser. I will appoint a chairwoman of the board.

Notes to the Leader

Make sure you're not making fun of the Jewish mother. You want the Jewish people in your group, and other nationalities in your group, to be able to laugh at themselves and not feel insulted. Do what you do with love and care. I'm Jewish, so I picked the Jewish mother. The group could see that I wouldn't be insulted and that the exercise can be done with humor and love.

Group Improvisation

We'll do the same improvisation of the Jewish mother and this time we'll be in a supermarket. We'll show all of the loving and admirable traits of the Jewish mother.

Group Improvisation

We'll do one more improvisation of a Jewish mother. This time you'll be at a parents' meeting. Tone down the stereotypical characteristics. You choose the characteristics that you'd like to be in this scene.

Feedback Session

How did it feel? What did you notice? As you can tell with the Jewish mother stereotype, there are many ways to do this person. As with any stereotype, you must understand WHY she is like she is. Find her vulnerability and soft spots. In a Neil Simon play called *Broadway Bound*, the mother is stern and difficult. However, at the end of the play, she dances with her son. It's a touching moment that shows her warmth and tenderness. It proves the point that every stereotype is multi-dimensional. We do stereotypes a great disservice if we only show and harp on one trait.

Variation 1

Pick another stereotype to become. Pick one trait to accentuate. Example: If your stereotype is an outrageous colorful Italian person, exaggerate it even more. We're in an airport. At the feedback session, have each person tell the stereotype they chose and which trait they picked to accentuate.

Notes to the Leader

I think it's important to do several traits in the stereotypes that your participants choose to do. Every character is multi-dimensional and they'll discover these dimensions when they do different parts of the stereotype.

Variation 2

Have your group do the same improvisation as in Variation 1, and pick another trait to accentuate in their character. In the feedback session, have each person share the stereotype they chose and what trait they picked to accentuate.

I could not exist without the music of nature's simplicity—whether it be the sighing of wind—
or the throbbing of the sea — or just the laughter of a little brook that wanders beside the Cider Mill road.
— Winston Abbott, writer

Nature
45-60 minutes

PURPOSE: Enhances sensitivity to nature
Helps break down inhibitions

Notes to the Leader

This exercise is best done outdoors.

Procedure

If you can't be outdoors, you can do the exercise indoors. Find your own space. Lie down and close your eyes. Be in a nature spot that you love. Feel it all around you. It is surrounding you. Feel your nature spot inside of your body. Become this nature spot. Feel it in your veins. Taste it, smell it, hear it, see it and touch it. Become one with this special nature spot.

Movement

Open your eyes and move around. Become the essence of your nature spot. Don't encounter each other. You can add sounds along with your movement.

Group Improvisation

You're on a nature walk. I'll be a guide for your group. Be your part of nature as you walk. Let it affect your body and voice. Freeze.

Group Improvisation

You're office workers and are sitting at your desks. Keep your nature spot with you. Each one of you should have an objective and action.

Feedback Session

How easy was it for you to create your nature spot? Could you become one with it? Could you carry the essence with you on the nature walk? Could you keep it with you in the office improvisation? What did you notice happening inside your body? Did it affect your voice? In what way did it affect your voice and body?

Having to play safe stunts any artist.
                                    — Uta Hagen

Mask Exercise
30-45 minutes

PURPOSE: Encourages silliness and quick-thinking
Enhances sense of humor and vulnerability

Notes to the Leader

In this exercise, it's important that you demonstrate some silly faces. When your group sees you being ridiculous, they'll feel safe to be silly.

This exercise is wonderful because many funny characters can be created in your group. Participants get out of themselves and are able to laugh at themselves.

Always remind them to keep their bodies relaxed as they take on different masks. They can send liquid to any body parts that feel restricted or tight. Their bodies must be flowing and relaxed.

Procedure

Let's all stand in a circle. We're going to exercise our faces. Move your jaw, tongue, eyebrows and forehead, and squinch it up. Make your face huge and wide. Open your eyes wide. Move your lips, nose and mouth. Wriggle it all around. Make crazy faces. Be as silly as you can.

When I clap my hands, make a frozen face. Let your face freeze in one position. You'll hold each position for about five seconds. We'll do many different faces. I'll clap my hands when I want you to freeze your face in one position.

Movement

Find your own space. When I clap my hands, I want you to make a face and hold that face. Then slowly let your body transform and move in a way that matches your face. Example: If you have a bright and huge smiley face, your body might start to move with huge and open movements. Go with the first impulses you feel when I clap my hands.

Feedback Session

What was this like for you? Did you feel silly? Did your body match your face?

The movement gives you an awareness of what it is to 'become' someone else. It brings out different parts of you. There is a theory that once you physically take on the movement of another person; you begin to feel what that person feels like INSIDE. You empathize with that person and understand why they behave the way they do. Example: You see a very slouched and sad person. His whole body expresses sadness. When you begin to move and imitate what he looks like, you begin to feel what he's feeling like inside.

You see a jolly person laughing hysterically. If you imitate him, you might begin to laugh and feel that person's humor and giddiness.

Group Improvisation

You're older hippies, around fifty to sixty years old. You're at a high school reunion. You're trying to figure out how to bring the 1960's back again. For you, they were the good old times. When I clap my hands, get a mask on your face and let your body change with your mask. You're now an older hippie. You carry that mask and body into the improvisation. See how your mask affects your voice. Keep your body and voice relaxed.

Feedback Session

Could you hold your mask? How did your mask affect your movement? How did your mask affect your voice?

Variation 1

We'll do the same *Mask Exercise*, but this time when I clap my hands, I want you to take your hands and **bring a mask to your face**. It will be like you are putting on a mask. Then you will move with the mask on. I'll demonstrate what I mean.

Variation 2

Each person will take a frozen mask when I clap my hands. Only your face will be involved. Your body will remain relaxed. You will talk to other people in the group, but hold your mask as you encounter each person.

Variation 3

As we do this exercise, I am going to divide the group in half so each group can watch the other half.

Variation 4

You will pick a mask that you would like to show to the world. Then we'll do a group improvisation with that mask. Use your face and body.

Variation 5

I pick a word and call it out to the group. Example: I call out the word "Angel." You all find a mask to match the word. You can also find a sound for your mask, if you like. Your body will change to fit your mask. You will create an autobiography of this person and do a group improvisation. After each improvisation, I will call out a new word. The next word might be "Monster" or "Oak tree." You take a frozen mask of whatever that word means to you. Your face and body will transform to the word I call out.

One word frees us of all the weight and pain of life. That word is love.
— Sophocles, Greek playwright

Person You Know Well Exercise
45-60 minutes

PURPOSE: Increases vulnerability
Promotes risk-taking

Notes to the Leader

Make sure you allow enough time for your group to ground and come back to reality after this exercise is completed. It is an exciting exercise and it can bring up intense emotions. Have a box of tissues available in case people cry.

Procedure

Find your own space in the room. Lie down and close your eyes. Trust the first image that you receive. Pick a person from your family or someone you know well and love. This person can be living or dead. See that person in detail. See the person's face. Feel that person's energy. Hear his or her laughter.

See some gestures that they do. See them in their environment. What objects, colors, people and animals are around the person? Hear this person's voice talking to you or to someone else. You might recreate a conversation you had with this person.

Why did you pick this person? Feel in your body the love you have or had for this person. If tears or laughter come, that's fine. See the person moving, walking and talking.

Feel the person enter your body. You're one with them. You're becoming this person. Feel totally relaxed. What would it be like to be with this person?

Put this person's essence inside your body, heart and soul. Feel this person inside you. How do they stand? What clothes do they wear? Put this person in one place doing one activity. How does this person do that particular activity? Feel this person's heart inside of you. How does this person interact with others?

Slowly come back to this space, this room. Stretch your body. Feel your face, your hands. Slowly, come to a sitting position and then come to a standing position.

Divide Into Pairs

Find a partner. Find someone you haven't worked with before. You're both the person you know well. Stand or sit and share something about your life with your partner. Switch so each person has a turn. Freeze.

Group Improvisation

You're now at a cocktail party, meeting other people in the room. You're this person you know well. Who might you talk to? Who might you ignore? What topics of conversation interest you?

Feedback Session

How did this feel? What did you learn? What did you notice? What surprised you? What happened that you didn't expect to happen? What were your interactions like?

Variation 1

Do the same exercise and become a famous person whom you admire.

Variation 2

Do the same exercise and become a person whom you don't like. By doing this exercise, you might develop empathy and compassion for this person. You will 'become' this person and may get some insights as to why this person is the way he/she is.

Variation 3

Do the same exercise. Pick a fairy tale character or cartoon character to become. This will enhance your silliness and child-like behavior.

S.M. Volkonski says if vowels are a river and consonants are the banks,
it is necessary to reinforce the latter lest there be floods.
— Constantin Stanislavksi, actor, theater director

Pick A Voice
30-60 minutes

PURPOSE: Increases body-awareness
Develops emotional range
Enhances vocal variety

Notes to the Leader

Stress to your group that they shouldn't strain their voices. They should use their voices gently and make sure they are breathing easily before each sound is made.

Procedure

Find your own space in the room. Close your eyes. Make a sound. You can make any sound at all. It can be a small sound or a large sound. Make the sound of an open vowel, such as *Ah* or *Oh*. Experiment with different sounds. How does this sound feel in your body? Relax your throat, jaw, tongue and lips. Feel the sound spread throughout your body. Check and make sure your body is relaxed. Open your eyes.

Movement

Start moving and keep your sound going. What does the sound do to your body? Use your body in small and large ways. Exaggerate your sound and see what your body does? Use different parts of your body with the sound. Put the sound in different parts of your body. Put the sound inside your hand, your fanny, and your chest. Experiment by making tiny sounds. Let your body follow with tiny gestures and motions.

Develop a walk. What is your rhythm, texture and energy? Keep the sounds going and base your walk on the sound. What is the energy of your walk? What is your essence as you move with your sound? As you continue walking, create an autobiography.

Group Improvisation

You're in a health food store. Don't talk to anyone at the beginning of the improvisation. Feel your sound in your body and see how it influences your movement. We'll add our voices in a few minutes.

Divide Into Pairs

Structure an improvisation based on the sound. Each person should have a different sound. Move together while each of you makes your sound. Then structure an improvisation where you can talk to each other. You can use the character that you have just created or create a new person. Make sure each person has an objective, action and obstacle. See Appendix J for Glossary of Terms.

Feedback Session

How did your voice feel? What was this like for you? Could you keep your body and voice relaxed while you did the improvisation? How did the sound influence your movement?

Those who know don't talk, those who talk don't know.

— Lao-tzu, founder of Taoism

Animal Image
30-45 minutes

PURPOSE: To increase movement vocabulary
To stretch self-image
To bond the group
To be vulnerable with each other

Notes to the Leader

This was one of the most valuable techniques I used when I was acting. People remind me of animals and it's wonderful to imitate people using animal qualities.

Procedure

Spread out in the room. Go with the first image you receive. Get an image of an animal you'd like to be. Slowly transform into that animal, one part at a time—hands, arms and face. Feel the outer qualities of the animal—fur, fins, feathers, teeth, lips, mouth and eyes. Feel what the animal feels like inside your body.

Move in your environment. Don't encounter anyone else. Eat as the animal eats. Sleep as your animal. Go to the bathroom as your animal. Do an activity that your animal does. Explore your environment.

Start to notice the other animals in the room. Meet the other animals if you can. Some animals you may not want to meet. Make sounds as your animals. Freeze.

In the next two to three minutes, pick one or two movement qualities that your animal has, and transform to a person doing those one or two qualities. Example: If you are bird, what qualities might you transfer to a person? You might primp and preen yourself. If you are a gorilla, you might move with huge cumbersome movements. How do you move? What is your walk like? How do you feel?

On a scale of one to ten, do the animal as a person at a number seven. Now do it a number two. Your movements may now be more internal. What you're doing is subtle. Blow it up to ten so you're over the top. Now bring it back to a number five.

Group Improvisation

You're in a personnel office waiting for an interview. Create an autobiography. You're not talking to anyone else. This is a silent improvisation. Keep one or two of the animal qualities while you wait. Freeze.

We're going to make a circle as students in this class. Keep the qualities of your animal. When we're in the circle, we'll go around and each person will tell the one or two qualities they chose to keep when they transformed from being an animal to a person.

Group Improvisation

Move around as your animals again. Explore your environment. Don't meet other animals. Pick two qualities of your animal and transform to a person. Freeze. You are now all firemen trying to raise money to buy a new truck. Keep one or two qualities of your animal while doing this improvisation.

Feedback Session

What was that like? How did it feel? What surprised you? What did you learn that you didn't know before?

Notes to the Leader

You can go to Appendix B: Suggestions for Two-Person Improvisations, and have your group do improvisations while keeping their animal qualities. It's valuable to have your group watch animals. They can visit the zoo and visit a pet store. They can see animals on the street and start imitating them and find out what the animal's essence feels like. Example: Follow a poodle and start walking like the poodle might walk if she were a person. What is the temperament of the poodle? How does she move? What does she think about? It's fun to watch people and see what animals they remind you of.

My choice of colors does not rest on any scientific theory;
it is based on observation, on feeling, on the experience of my sensibility.

— Henri Matisse, artist

Three Imitate Three
30-45 minutes

PURPOSE: Teaches observational skills
Improves observational skills
Teaches spotlighting

Procedure

Three people will volunteer to do an improvisation. I'll tell you who you are and where you are. Everyone in the class watches the improvisation. Example: You are all athletic trainers who work out together. You are sharing your skills and what you feel are the most important things to know in a workout.

Notes to the Leader

After the improvisation is completed, pick three people from the group to do the exact same improvisation, exactly the way the three people did it. From that point on, the class will be more alert and watch closely to see what happens in the improvisation. They can then select whom they would like to imitate when other people get up in front of the group to do the improvisation.

Feedback Session

What qualities did the people capture who imitated the first group? What worked well? What essences of the person did each person capture?

Faith is to believe what we do not see; the reward of faith is to see what we believe.

— St. Augustine

Conditioning Forces
30-45 minutes

PURPOSE: To give participants other techniques to use in improvisations
Heightens imagination skills
Creates group ensemble

Procedure

We'll be doing a series of improvisations with Conditioning Forces. A conditioning force is a condition that influences how you move, feel and communicate. Example: It's a hot day. Your clothes stick to you. You might be wiping your sweat from your face. It is hard to concentrate. You move and talk at a slower pace.

Everyone spread out in the room. Conditioning forces may involve sense memories. Here is a wonderful quote: "The art of being convincing is being convinced." If you believe in the conditioning force, we'll believe it. I will say a conditioning force and you will let it affect you. You're not relating to anyone else in the room.

It's a hot day.
It's a freezing cold day.
You're in a hurry.
You have a stomachache.
You have athlete's foot.
You smell something unpleasant.

Notes to the Leader

Have your group make a list of conditioning forces. You can use this list when you do the improvisations. Examples: foot blister, hard of hearing, hungry, car alarm going off outside the room, shoes are too tight, bad breath, itchy insect bite.

Three-Person Improvisation

Three people are sitting in a park on a Sunday afternoon. Each person is elderly. Each one has a conditioning force. One person has a cold. One person is slightly deaf. One has trouble breathing. Tell your group where they are and who they are.

After a few people have done the exercise, you can let the members pick their own conditioning force.

Procedure

Divide into groups of three or four people. Decide on a place for the improvisation, who you are and what conditioning force each person has. You'll have ten minutes to rehearse it and then each group will perform their improvisation for the group. If certain things change when you do the improvisation before the group, that's fine. The most important thing is you know where you are, who you are, and that you let the conditioning force affect you.

Feedback Session

How did it feel? What did you notice? How did the conditioning force affect you?

It's not important what you know. It's important what you don't know and discover.
— Carlo Mazzone-Clementi, actor, teacher, director, mime

Inanimate Quality
30-60 minutes

PURPOSE: To increase movement vocabulary
To use your imagination
To build an ensemble in your group

Notes to the Leader

There are six different exercises using inanimate qualities. You can choose to do each one and build upon each exercise. Or you may select to do just one or two of the exercises.

With each exercise, remind your group of the following important things: Keep your body relaxed. Keep breathing. Vary your rhythms with each quality. Use different levels, i.e. being on the floor, sitting or standing.

Exercise One

Procedure

Find your own space in the room. Close your eyes. I'm going to say a word and I want you to move one body part however *that word makes you feel*. You can experiment moving different body parts in this exercise. Stay in one place as you do this exercise. Remember to keep your body relaxed as you are moving.

Gooey — Freeze — Come back to neutral.
Clouds — Freeze — Come back to neutral.
Fudge — Freeze — Come back to neutral.
Hot wax — Freeze — Come back to neutral.
Chocolate pudding — Freeze — Come back to neutral.
Rubbery — Freeze — Come back to neutral.
Sandpaper — Freeze — Come back to neutral.
Broken glass — Freeze — Come back to neutral.

Now you can open your eyes and use your whole body. Move through space as I say each word. Be respectful of everyone's space. You're not interacting with anyone. You're moving as if you are alone.

Notes to the Leader

Repeat the same sequence, starting with Gooey and ending with Broken glass.

Procedure

Now you'll interact with each other non-verbally. Find the rhythm of each quality. What does the rhythm of each quality feel like in your body? You are moving to each quality, and moving in silence.

Notes to the Leader

Repeat the same sequence starting with Gooey and ending with Broken glass.

Procedure

Find your own space again. Close your eyes. I'll say each word. Please talk softly, using the voice with the quality I give you. You can say whatever you feel like, putting the qualities of the word in your voice.

Notes to the Leader

Repeat the same sequence starting with Gooey and ending with Broken glass.

Procedure

We'll do group improvisations with each quality. I'll give you the place and tell you who you are, and you'll move around and talk to each other. Keep the qualities in your voice and body.

Notes to the Leader

Repeat the same sequence starting with Gooey and ending with Broken glass. You can pick the place of each improvisation. Examples: Classroom. You are college kids waiting for the teacher to enter. Train Station. You are commuters waiting for your train. High School Prom. You are seniors and this is your prom.

Feedback Session

How did this feel? What did you notice? How did you manifest each inanimate quality?

Exercise Two

Procedure

We're going to move through these different textures as a group. Notice how your body moves. Remember to keep your body relaxed as you're moving. You can encounter others, or you can move in your own space.

Boulders of stone — Freeze — Come back to neutral.
Whipped cream — Freeze — Come back to neutral.
Lace — Freeze — Come back to neutral.
Crepe paper — Freeze — Come back to neutral.
Snow storm — Freeze — Come back to neutral.
Stardust — Freeze — Come back to neutral.
Spaghetti — Freeze — Come back to neutral.

Feedback Session

What was that like? How did it feel? Did you have any new insights?

Exercise Three

Procedure

Let's make a huge list of inanimate qualities.

Notes to the Leader

Use a big flip-chart and write with large print so everyone can read it easily.

Procedure

We'll do two-person improvisations and I'll tell you where you are and who you are. You'll choose which inanimate quality you would like to be. You'll use your voice and body with the essence of this quality. Example: You are athletes in the locker room and trying out for the Olympic swim team.

Exercise Four

Procedure

Divide into two's and three's. Decide on where you are and who you are. Try on at least three different inanimate qualities as you rehearse your improvisation. You'll have twenty minutes to rehearse. Each improvisation is three to five minutes.

Notes to the Leader

Go around to each group and watch. If they are stuck or not sure how to proceed, you can ask them questions. After each improvisation, you can coach and ask them to be a different movement quality. Try to expand each person's movement vocabulary and challenge everyone to move in new and different ways.

Exercise Five

Procedure

Spread out in the room. Find your own space. Do a task with one inanimate quality. Example: The task might be to comb your hair, brush your teeth, put on your shoes, exercise, find something in your pocket, or wash the dishes. Personify one inanimate quality as you do your task.

Exercise Six

Procedure

Find a partner. This exercise is for personifying the vocal quality of the inanimate object. You're free to move your body too, if that helps you get the vocal qualities in your voice.

Have a conversation using one inanimate quality. Example: Being gooey. Find a new partner and have another conversation while being broken glass.

Notes to the Leader

Have your group switch partners five times. Ask them to share certain things in each conversation. Example: Talk about a dream of something you would love to do in your life. Talk about what you are doing this weekend.

Assignment

Do observations with people in public and notice what inanimate qualities they personify in their movements and voice. Be aware that a person's body can move like whipped cream, but that her voice might be like porcupine quills.

Notes to the Leader

The following is a list of inanimate objects you can use for this exercise:

tar	sandpaper	mud
water	cactus needles	blood
hard	windy	finger paints
flour	burnt match	Silly Putty®
sand	latex	gravel
gritty	chrome	petroleum jelly
cotton	Teflon®	granite
slippery	hair	tears
sticky	brass	hay
cold	Crisco®	bubbly
prickly	cold water	shiny
frozen	ice cube	smooth
steamy	popsicle	thick
needles	feathers	dirty
perfume	feather bed	messy
limp	sunlight	rough
greasy	moonlight	crackly
powder	rose petals	prickly
chalk	polyester	Spanish moss
sharp	tissue	seaweed
wood chips	cotton balls	salt water
thorny	sneeze	razor blades
silky	toothpaste	rust
shiny	foam	bark
Jell-O	soap	petals
dirty sock	whipped cream	soft
wet	quicksand	bright

When I was in Jerusalem for three months, I knew an Israeli landlady in her fifties. Her TV was broken and she called the repairman. It took him four visits to fix the screen. But you knew even before he came the first time what was wrong. He could have brought the correct tube and fixed it immediately. She looked at me in astonishment. Yes, but then we couldn't have had a relationship, sat and drunk tea and discussed the progress of the repairs. Of course, the goal is not to fix a machine but to have relationships.

— Natalie Goldberg, author

Object Exercise
60-90 minutes

PURPOSE: Builds concentration
Promotes commitment to follow through and go for what you really want
Inspires your imagination

Notes to the Leader

Stress that there is no violence in this exercise.

Procedure

Find an object that you can hold in your hand. It can be a shoe, watch, brush, etc. Find your own space in the room and sit down with your object. Look at it and study it. Notice its details. Take it apart if you can. Smell it . . . taste it . . . listen to it.

Close your eyes and feel your object again. Smell it . . . taste it . . . touch it . . . listen to it. Explore the object in every possible way you can with your eyes closed.

Open your eyes and look at your object again. I want you to *pretend that this object means more to you than anything in the world.* How would you feel about it? Create an autobiography around your object. Who gave it to you? Did you find the object? Did you buy it? How long have you had it? Where do you keep it? How do you use this object?

Let's make a large circle and sit down. Two people will go into the center of the circle. I may send both people in the center of the circle with their objects. Or, I may ask one of you to leave your object outside of the circle and not bring it with you into the center of the circle.

Your objective is to get the other person's object. If your partner does not have his object, you want your own object. If you both have objects, you each want the other person's object. There is no right or wrong way to do this exercise. There is NO violence. That's important to hear.

The last rule is that you MUST do this exercise without talking. Don't mime, "I want your object." Just see how you can get the other person's object. It will be fascinating to see what happens with each pair that goes into the circle. I only send two people in the center at a time. Each couple will be in the center for ten to fifteen minutes. I'll end the exercise. Even if both people still have their objects, that's fine. I'll sense when the exercise is complete.

It's important for those of us watching to be quiet and pay attention. This is an observation exercise for all of us. The back and shoulders are the most expressive part of the body, so it doesn't matter if you can't see both people's faces.

Notes to the Leader

You might have to remind people not to mime or indicate in pantomime that they want the other person's object. They often try to mime it with hand motions and acting it out in some way.

The focus is intense for each person. The people watching will feel the focus and concentration of the people in the center of the circle. Your group will learn to go after something they really want.

Feedback Session

How did it feel? What did you see happening between the two people in the center of the circle? How did you respond when the other person wanted your object? How did you feel about your own object? What did you learn?

Assignment

Watch three people during the next week. These people should be trying to get something from another person. Watch how they go about getting what they want, either verbally or non-verbally. Babies are perfect people to watch for this kind of observation.

I love to think that the day you're born, you're given the world as your birthday present.
— Leo Buscaglia, author

Emotion Memory Exercises
45-60 minutes

PURPOSE: To bond your group
To let participants have accessibility to their emotions
Increases vulnerability

Procedure

The following exercises help you to get in touch with your emotions. If you want to feel joy during the day, you can re-experience an emotion or recollections of joy and you'll begin to re-experience that joyous feeling. *An emotion memory is remembering a time in your past when you felt a certain emotion.* You see and feel as many of the details as you can. You see the place, who was there, the colors, textures and feelings you had. Your senses also come into play: smells, tastes and sounds.

It's important that your emotion recollections are private. We are sharing some of these memories here, but for the most part you never tell anyone what images and recollections you use.

Notes to the Leader

There are many exercises listed for emotion and sense memory. Pick the ones you'd like to use. Remember to tell your group about confidentiality. What is shared in the group stays in the group. The participants will feel safer, be more vulnerable and willing to share more. When you do these exercises, always pick an upbeat emotion as the last emotion they experience at the end of the exercise.

Tell your group that if they experience a feeling that's too intense, they can let it go and find another experience. Tell them they are in charge of what emotions they choose and how deeply they go into that emotion.

Participants pick partners for different parts of the exercise. You say, "The person with the shortest hair goes first," or "The person with the bigger feet goes first," or "The person wearing the brightest colors goes first." It's fun to make up silly things so they'll be more relaxed when they start the exercise.

Exercise One

Procedure

Find a space. Lie down on the floor. We'll take one minute for each emotion.

Get an image for each word I say. Go with the first image you receive. Breathe.

Remember a time when you felt totally exhilarated. Where were you? Who was there? Where do you feel it in your body? What happened?

Notes to the Leader

Take your group through many emotion recollections — frenzy, grief, humiliation, love, shyness, peace. Always ask the following questions after each emotion: Where were you? Who was there? Where do you feel it in your body? What happened?

Procedure

Remember a time when you were excited. Find a partner and share that time with your partner. Each person will have three minutes to share.

Exercise Two

Make a circle. Close your eyes. Remember a time of incredible joy. Feel it in your body. See the place where you were. See the people who are present. Be there. Open your eyes. Share one word from your experience. We'll go around the circle five times. If you'd like, you can come to the center of circle and do a gesture or movement with your emotion.

Exercise Three

Find a partner. This time we are going to do a scene. The scene is as follows:

A: Hi.
B: Hi.
A: I missed you.
B: I missed you, too.

Decide who will be A and who will be B. Both of you use the emotion recall of sad when you do the scene. Get an image and say your line.

Now A, be excited and B, be bored.

Now A, be embarrassed and B, be nervous.

How did this feel? Could you access the images from your emotion recollections?

Exercise Four

Stand in a circle. Close your eyes. Go with the first image you receive. I'll say a feeling or emotion and I'd like you to remember a time in your life when you felt this emotion.

I'll go around and tap each person and you will say just one word about the emotion. Then I'll say another emotion and I would like you to remember a time when you felt that emotion. I'll go around again and tap each person and you can say one word about that emotion.

Between each emotion, get an image of a tree, which is rooted and grounded. Come back to neutral between each emotion that I mention. In neutral, you are a blank slate, so you can experience each emotion in a fresh way.

Notes to the Leader

It's important for the leader to be sensitive to the group and allow about forty to sixty seconds per emotion. Here are some suggestions for emotions to use: sadness, excitement, love, nervousness, stubbornness, embarrassment, boredom and silliness.

.

Exercise Five

Find a partner and sit down across from them. I'll hand out a list of emotions and your partner will say one word to you and give you thirty seconds to have an emotion recollection. I'll ring a bell softly when it's time to go on to the next emotion. Decide who is A and who is B. I would like the person who is A to close your eyes. The person who is B will now read each emotion. There is no conversation between you. You are just remembering a time when you felt that emotion. Remember, I'll ring the bell when it's time to go the next emotion. If an experience comes to you that is too intense, let it go and find another experience. Remember, you're in charge.

Ambition, bliss, bitterness, boredom, calm, depression, embarrassment, exhaustion, grief, hate, joy, jealousy, lust, numbness, overwhelm, patience, rage, stillness, snobbishness, fear, vulnerability, security.

Switch and let A read the emotions to B. Discuss with your partner what the experience was like for you.

Exercise Six

Find a partner. Sit across from each other. Decide who is A and who is B.

A: Share a time with your partner that you were blissful. Switch. Share a time you were scared. Switch. Share a time when you felt shy. Switch. Share a time when you felt beautiful or handsome. Switch. Share a time when you felt euphoric. Switch.

Feedback Session

How did this feel? What was this like for you? What did you notice? What did you learn?

An act of imagination is what makes being alive possible.
— Michael Shurtleff

Sense Memory Exercises
45-60 minutes

PURPOSE: To bond your group
To let participants have accessibility to their emotions
Increases vulnerability

Procedure

Sense memories are memories involving sight, taste, sound, touch and smell. Emotion memories usually have sense memories within them. Sense memories frequently have emotion memories associated with them. To have an image, is to have a body change. You'll feel interesting things happening in your body as you experience sense memories.

We're going to do a series of exercises to get you in touch with many different types of sense memories.

It's important that your emotion and sense memories are private. We are sharing some of these memories, but for the most part, you never tell anyone what images and recollections you use.

Exercise One

Procedure

Find a place on the floor. Lie down. Relax your body. We'll do a series of sense memories.
Touch: feel a cat or dog
Hear: a crackling fire
Smell: hot fudge
Taste: your favorite ice cream or food
See: an ocean view
Touch: something or someone you love
Hear: something you love
Smell: something you love
Taste: something you love
See: something you love
Stand up. Make a circle. Each one of you can share one of your sense memories.

Exercise Two

Procedure

Go around the circle and each person say "Hi" with the sense memory of something or someone you love. Notice how it affects your body and voice.

Exercise Three

Procedure

Make a circle. Remember something that happened today that involved one of your senses- taste, sight, touch, sound or smell. Re-experience it.

Go around the circle and share your memory in one sentence.

Exercise Four

Procedure

Remember a time when you felt hungry. Where do you feel it in your body? Remember a time when you felt hot. What parts of your body feel hot? Remember a time when you felt cold. Where specifically do you feel cold? Remember a time when you heard something wonderful. Remember a time when you felt a wonderful sensation.

Exercise Five

Procedure

Everyone find a chair to sit on or you can lie on the floor. Close your eyes.

Pretend you're in a waiting room, as if you were being rained on.

Pretend you're in an airport and smell some rotting meat.

Pretend you're at a bus stop and feel the cold wind on your face.

Pretend you're in a train station and it is ninety-eight degrees.

Pretend you have on a sweater that itches you.

Pretend you're in a hotel and the fire alarm goes off.

Pretend you're in a department store and your favorite piece of music comes on the loud speaker.

Group Improvisation

You're at the zoo. Pick any sense memory you wish and relate to people there, but keep the sense memory in your body. It will affect how you speak and move.

Exercise Six

Procedure

Find a partner. Stand across from your partner. Close your eyes. Taste something wonderful. Open your eyes and each of you say to each other, "You look wonderful."

Smell something that is unpleasant. Say to your partner, "It's nice seeing you."

Touch something soft. Say to your partner, "I've had a great day."

See something strange. Say to your partner, "I just lost my job."

Hear something beautiful. Say to your partner, "I'm going on vacation."

How do these images affect your voice?

Exercise Seven

Procedure

Find a partner. Here's your script.

A: Come here.

B: I don't want to.

A: Please.

B: All right.

A's use the sense recall of seeing a beautiful sight.

B's use the sense recall of seeing something upsetting.

Notes to the Leader

Brainstorm with your group to create a list of sense memories and write them on a large sheet of newsprint.

Exercise Eight

Procedure

We're going to do an improvisation with sense recall. Look at the list we just made, and pick one you would like to use.

1. You are at a neighborhood meeting to discuss people cleaning up after their dogs. Each person will use one sense recall as they do the improvisation.
2. You are models in a dressing room getting ready for the fashion show.
3. You're business executives at a meeting, trying to figure out how to plan the best holiday party ever.

The problem is not to be convincing but to be convinced.
— Stella Adler, acting teacher

Advanced Exercises

Best Physical Parts
45-90 minutes

PURPOSE: Builds self-esteem and confidence
Heightens self-awareness and awareness of others

Notes to the Leader

Remind your group not to judge this exercise. Ask them to remain a child, be silly and have fun. Especially in finding our worst parts, you don't want the exercise to get too heavy. If you have a sense of lightness as you lead it, your group will trust their impulses and let their spontaneity flow easily.

Procedure

Find your own space in the room. Lie down and close your eyes. Make sure you have enough room around you. Let your body relax. Feel your breath going in and out easily. Please go with the first image that comes in. Trust that image. What is your best physical part of your body? Let that one part fill up your whole body. Become one with that part. Slowly come to a standing position.

Movement

Move around as that best physical part. What does it feel like? What do you notice? Exaggerate the movement. How is your movement different? Go back to a normal way of moving this physical part.

Notes to the Leader

Encourage your group to exaggerate that one body part. If one man's favorite part is his biceps, tell him to let his whole body become his biceps.

Group Improvisation

You're all at a bus stop waiting for a bus. Be your best physical part. You may choose to talk or be silent. This is up to you. Notice how you move and relate.

Procedure

Lie down again. Close your eyes. Go with the first image that comes in. Now be your best emotional part. Let it fill your whole body. Become one with this emotional part. It fills you up. Stand up.

Movement

Move around the space as this best emotional part. You can add sound as you move around the space. Don't relate to anyone else in the room. Have fun with this part.

Group Improvisation

You're at a supermarket as your best emotional part. You can talk to others or remain quiet. How do you move? How does your movement affect your voice? What do you notice about how you are moving?

Procedure

Lie down again. Close your eyes. Go with the first image that comes in. What is your best mental trait? Let your whole body become that mental trait. It fills your whole body. It consumes your body. You and this mental trait are one.

Movement

Stand up and move around the room as this mental trait. Be respectful of each other's space as you move in the room. What does it feel like to move as this mental trait?

Group Improvisation

You're at an opening for an art gallery. You can talk to others or remain quiet. How do you move? What do you choose to talk about? Your whole body is reflecting this mental trait.

Procedure

Lie down one more time. You can pick one of the traits we have just done. You can be your best physical part, your best emotional part, or your best mental trait. Become one of those traits again. Let that part consume you from head to foot. You are that one part. Create an autobiography.

Group Improvisation

I'm going to appoint someone from the group to be a tour guide and take you on a tour. You're going to accentuate and be whatever BEST part you picked. The tour guide will give a tour of whatever she wishes. You can choose to talk to others or remain alone. That depends on your autobiography. Each of you will pick your one best part — physical, emotional or mental trait — with your body and voice.

Example: If your best part is your nose, you could stick it out even farther and show it off to the group.

Feedback Session

How did it feel? What did you notice? What part did you pick? What did you notice about each other? What did you learn? How was your posture? What was your voice like? What differences did you notice in your pace and rhythm? How did you hold your body? How did you handle objects?

What was your thought process? Was it different than it usually is? What were your gestures like? How did your body and parts of your body feel? Was your body held tight or was it loose and free in movement? What was your voice like? Where was your body center? How did you relate to each other? Did you touch each other? What was your subtext or thoughts behind what you were saying? Did you notice how many different colors you have in your personality?

Assignment

Watch people and see how they use their voice and body. How do they show you which part of themselves they like the best — physical, emotional or mental?

Creativity requires you turn off all judgment.
— Unknown

Worst Physical Parts
45-90 minutes

PURPOSE: Encourages taking off the mask
Encourages breaking down inhibitions

Notes to the Leader

Before you begin this second part of the exercise, make sure that you tell your group the following:

1. Have fun.
2. Enjoy it.
3. These worst parts have a lot of *energy and passion*.
4. It's important to get in touch with different sides of our personalities, our darker parts, or the parts of our personalities that we may not like. By becoming these parts, we'll make friends with them. You'll begin to love these parts. Through this exercise you'll develop compassion for these parts.

Procedure

Find your own space in the room. Lie down and close your eyes. Make sure you have enough room around you. Let your body relax. Feel your breath going in and out easily. Please go with the first image that comes in. Trust that image. What is your worst physical part of your body, or the part of your body you like the least? Let that one part fill up your whole body. Become one with that part. Slowly come to a standing position.

Movement

Move around as that worst physical part. What does it feel like? What do you notice? Exaggerate the movement. How is your movement different? Go back to a normal way of moving this physical part.

Notes to the Leader

Encourage your group to exaggerate that one body part. If one man's worst part is his feet, tell him to let his whole body become his feet.

Group Improvisation

You're all at a bus stop waiting for a bus. Be your worst part. You may choose to talk or be silent. This is up to you. Notice how you move and relate.

Procedure

Lie down again. Close your eyes. Go with the first image that comes in. Now be your worst emotional part. Let it fill your whole body. Become one with this emotional part. It fills you up. Stand up.

Movement

Move around the space as this worst emotional part. You can add sound as you move around the space. Don't relate to anyone else in the room. Have fun with this part.

Group Improvisation

You're at a supermarket as your worst emotional part. You can talk to others or remain quiet. How do you move? How does you movement affect your voice? What do you notice about how you are moving?

Procedure

Lie down again. Close your eyes. Go with the first image that comes in. What is your worst mental trait? Let your whole body become that mental trait. It fills your whole body. It consumes your body. You and this mental trait are one.

Movement

Stand up and move around the room as this mental trait. Be respectful of each other's space as you move in the room. What does it feel like to move as this mental trait?

Group Improvisation

You're at an opening for an art gallery. You can talk to others or remain quiet. How do you move? What do you choose to talk about? Your whole body is reflecting this mental trait.

Procedure

Lie down one more time. You can pick one of the traits we have just done. You can be your worst physical part, your worst emotional part, or your worst mental trait. Become one of those traits again. Let that part consume you from head to foot. You are that one part. Create an autobiography.

Group Improvisation

I'm going to appoint someone from the group to be a tour guide and take you on a tour. You're going to accentuate and be whatever WORST part you picked. The tour guide will give a tour of whatever she wishes. You can choose to talk to others or remain alone. That depends on your autobiography. Each of you will be your worst physical, emotional, or mental trait, with your body and voice.

An example might be, if your worst part is your nose, you could stick it out even farther and show it off to the group.

Feedback Session

How did it feel? What did you notice? What part did you pick for your worst physical part, your worst emotional part, and your worst mental trait? What did you notice about each other? What did you learn? How was your posture? What was your voice like? What differences did you notice in your pace and rhythm? How did you hold your body? How did you handle objects?

What was your thought process? Was it different than it usually is? What were your gestures like? How did your body and parts of your body feel? Was your body held tight or was it loose and free in movement? What was your voice like? Where was your body center? How did you relate to each other? Did you touch each other? What was your subtext or thoughts behind what you were saying? Did you notice how many different colors you have in your personality?

Assignment

Watch people and see how they use their voice and body. Do they hide from you the part of themselves that they don't like, either physical, emotional or mental?

In order to see the beauty, it is essential that we allow ourselves to be touched by things and by people, and that we be able to identify ourselves with them. All barriers between us and the world have to go, when looking at the beauty of a flower or listening to music, we are no longer ourselves: we become the flower, we become the music.
— Piero Ferrucci

Being Someone Opposite From You
45-90 minutes

PURPOSE: Increases vulnerability

Develops compassion for people unlike yourself

Encourages letting go of judges

Notes to the Leader

Prejudices form early in life. People have their likes and dislikes for certain kinds of people. In this exercise, people identify their likes and dislikes and become more empathetic towards people unlike themselves.

Procedure

Let's form a large circle. Close your eyes. Let your body relax. Go with the first image that enters your body. Get in touch with your breath going in and out.

What is the most opposite kind of person you could ever be? What kind of person is so far away from you, that you could never, in your wildest dreams, imagine becoming him or her? Go with the first image you receive. Find that person in your body. Feel this person joining you in your body. Open your eyes.

Movement

How does this person move? Create an autobiography for this person. What is this person's life like? Move as this person who is opposite from you. Walk around the room. What is your internal rhythm as you move? What is your external rhythm as you move? Don't relate to anyone else in the room. You're in your own space. Be respectful of other people's spaces.

Divide Into Pairs

Find someone whom you don't know well or haven't worked with in the group. As your opposite character, share something about yourself from your childhood. You can make it up or what you share might have some reality to it.

Group Improvisation

You're alone at a dance, as your character. You can choose to talk to others or remain quiet.

Feedback Session

What was this like? Who did each of you choose to become? What was the easiest part for you? What was the most challenging part? Did anything happen that surprised you?

Variation

I'd like each of you to pick a phrase or sentence that this person would say. We'll stand in a circle. We'll go around the circle and each person will say his phrase or sentence. As you say your sentence, let your body become this character's body. Stand as this person stands.

The group will imitate how you say your sentence. You'll say the sentence three times, then stop and watch us imitate you. We'll analyze your movement — head tilt, chest in, hip out and so on. It will be wonderful to imitate each other. We're not making fun of each other, just imitating what we see each person do.

Notes to the Leader

At our *Perfect People Party* each person chooses a character to be: a rich lady, a bum, a banker and so on. It is wonderful to portray someone unlike yourself. This exercise is similar, but done spontaneously, with people thinking on their feet, without planning whom they will be.

Assignment

Watch people and follow people whom are very different from you. Create your own autobiography of the people you follow. Try to put yourself inside them as you watch them. You'll be able to understand and see what makes them tick. You'll also develop compassion and understand more clearly why they do what they do.

You are the creator; whatever you think, that is what you create and that is what you become.

— Yogi Amrit Desai, spiritual teacher

You as a Child, Teen, Twenties, and Your Fantasy Age Exercise
45-90 minutes

PURPOSE: Increases self-awareness and acceptance
Create a bond between group participants

TOOLS: Drawing board
Newsprint paper - 18" x 24"
Crayons and markers

Notes to the Leader

This can be a powerful exercise. Make sure you have plenty of time to process the exercise.

Procedure

Find your own space and lie down. Close your eyes and relax your body. Feel your breath going in and out. Let in any sounds in the room or outside of the room. Don't block anything out. Remember a time when you were a child. You're four or five years old.

1. What was your favorite place or room?
2. What were its colors and textures?
3. What were you doing in that place?
4. Did you have any playmates or were you alone?
5. What were you like as a child?
6. What were your favorite games to play?
7. What did you look like?
8. How did people, such as your parents, teachers and friends, treat you?
9. What were your favorite clothes to wear?
10. What did you not like doing as a child?
11. What did you love doing?
12. What was a peak experience for you?
13. If someone were being you, what would they have to know about you?
14. What was an exciting memory from childhood?

Advance to your teenage years. Be you as a teenager, age thirteen, fourteen or fifteen. Get an image.
1. How did you feel being a teenager?
2. What were your friends like?
3. What do you remember looking like as a teenager?
4. What were your favorite things to do?
5. Were you alone or with friends?

Advance to your early twenties.
1. What memories stand out?
2. How did your body change?
3. Did your emotions change?
4. What are the special events that happened in your early twenties?
5. Relive one event.
6. See that event in as much detail as possible.
7. How is it different from when you were a child or teenager?
8. Who are you now — emotionally, physically, spiritually and mentally?
9. If someone were acting you, what would they have to know about you?

Advance to your thirties or forties.
1. Are you happy?
2. What activities do you like to do?
3. What do you look like?
4. How do you feel?
5. What is a peak experience you've had?

Slowly come to the present time.
1. What are you like now?
2. If you had to describe yourself to someone, what would you say?
3. What are peak experiences for you?
4. What do you love to do?
5. What drives you crazy?
6. What are some dreams that you have?

Slowly come back to this space. Feel your body on the floor. Feel your face, feel your hands. Stretch your body. Slowly come back to this space. Open your eyes.

Symbolic Drawing

Get some paper and crayons. Fold your paper into quarters. Work with one section of your folded paper at a time. Please remember to use your non-dominant hand when you draw. See page 30 for why we draw with our non-dominant hand.

Close your eyes — Get an image of what you were like as a child — Draw it.
Close your eyes — Get an image of what you were like as a teenager — Draw it.
Close your eyes — Get an image of what you were like as a person in your early twenties — Draw it.
Close your eyes — Get an image of what you were like as a person in your thirties or forties — Draw it.
Close your eyes — Get an image of who you are now — Draw it.

Divide Into Pairs

Share your drawings. Talk about what the experience was like for you. What did you notice? The person who listens can ask you questions, but shouldn't interpret your drawings. You'll each have ten minutes to share your drawings with each other.

Notes to the Leader

As people share their drawings, you can say, "Stop, are you saying what you want to say? Would you like to go deeper?"

Feedback Session

What was the exercise like for you? What did you notice about each age that you were? What was it like to do the symbolic drawings? What did you learn?

Variation

In another session, you could go more in depth and have group improvisations at each age — child, teen, twenties, thirties and forties. Participants could rediscover their younger selves if you wanted to extend the exercise in movement.

Notes to the Leader

The traits listed on the following page are not all of the traits that describe a child, a middle-aged person, or an old person. A child might also be tense, afraid, and so on. Have your group come up with their own words for each age you wish to do in this exercise.

Child	Middle-aged	Old
light	conscious	slow
loose	deliberate	frustrated
spontaneous	responsible	careful
weightless	painful	afraid
playful	separate from bodies	not confident
open	more careful	limited
unaffected	opposite of spontaneous	fearful
uninhibited	think before speak	shaky
quick	set	melancholy
playful	serene	slow thinking
trusting	aware of self in a different way	transitions slowly
not self-conscious	self-constricting	peaceful
high energy	habits of movement	not hurried
never stop moving	inhibited	gentle
helpless	in touch with mortality	sedate
proud	tense	poor vision
totally into themselves	responsibility weighs them down	poor hearing
do exactly what they want	poised	cautious
transform easily	dignified	sick
totally in their body	confident	tentative
fluid in their change	assured	always ready to fall
fearless	safe	stiff-jointed
not embarrassed	authority	
clumsy	caring	
awkward	caring what people think	
uncoordinated	worn down	

People are frightened of theatre because it is the nearest thing to talking and touching each other,
which is the deepest flash. In the ladder of artificiality, theatre is on the lowest rung.
— Heathcote Williams, English poet, actor and playwright

Song and Dance
30-45 minutes

PURPOSE: Encourages ability to take risks
Diagnostic tool for the leader
Develops movement vocabulary
Stimulates thinking on your feet

Notes to the Leader

This exercise is one of the best diagnostic tools I use when leading a group. It tells me the following things about a student:

1. A person's self-image
2. What they need to work on in the group and in their life
3. How accessible they are to their emotions
4. How easily they can think and act on their feet
5. If they can be in the moment and let go of the past character they were doing
6. How vulnerable they are

In this exercise, you must trust your insights and intuitions. You'll be working one to one with each person. You can coach each person for ten to fifteen minutes and give feedback for about ten minutes. As you coach them to do different things, try not to censor what your intuition tells you to suggest. See yourself as an open channel and let in your insights and intuition. Trust the voices that you hear.

In this exercise, I let people volunteer. You'll assign the exercise a week before you start coaching the first person. Say to the group, "I would like you to bring in a song to sing to the group. The song can be *Happy Birthday.* Any song you bring in is fine. You don't have to be a good singer to do this exercise."

If no one volunteers to do this exercise, just wait. Someone will eventually go to the front of the room. I suggest you let two people do this exercise per meeting. The rest of your class time is for group ensemble work. It may take ten weeks for everyone in your group to do the exercise. It's well worth it. You can start doing the exercise during the third or fourth meeting.

As the person sings his song, you'll be suggesting different ways for him to do the song. After the person sings his song one or two times, I might tell him to just say the words of the song, and not to sing it. I might say, "Keep singing the song, but do it as a go-go dancer in a nightclub. Now talk the song. Be a light bulb. Now be a table. Be a little boy saying 'good-bye' to your best friend. Sing the song being a cloud. Now say the words of the song and this time, be at the funeral of your best friend. Do the song as a baboon." Suggest to the person singing that they use the group, i.e. if you ask them to be a go-go dancer in a nightclub, have the group be patrons in the nightclub.

Tell them to trust their instincts. The important thing is that you NOT give them time to think. Give one direction, let them do it for ten seconds, or thirty seconds and then quickly jump in with another suggestion. You don't have to let them complete the whole song. They might say two sentences and then you can give them another direction. Remind them that there is no right or wrong way to do this exercise.

Procedure

I'll be coaching each person for about ten to fifteen minutes. You'll just sing your song. The point of the exercise is not to see how well you sing. I'll ask you to do various things as you sing your song. That's it. The rest of the group should remain quiet and attentive. This helps the person who is working. When we're finished, I'll ask someone in the group to take notes on what I say to you. The reason someone else does this is so you and I can talk to each other and you don't have to be bothered taking notes. Don't just listen to my words, but watch me, and you'll understand what I am saying. The main reason I have another person take notes is so that the person up front and I can look at each other. The energy that passes between us is crucial.

Feedback Session

Someone in the group volunteers to take notes for the person who just worked. I'll be telling you what I saw, what worked well, your strong points and also areas for you to work on.

Notes to the Leader

It's important that you speak to each person in a personal and caring way. Give the critique with love and respect. The purpose of the critique is to open people up to themselves, to help them grow and expand their creativity and imagination, and to encourage them to be bold and take risks. You'll see many ways that each person can grow.

Many breakthroughs happen in this exercise or soon after the exercise is finished. The reason this happens is because people take risks and are receptive during the critiques.

Always start by saying something positive. Example: "You have a wonderful presence up there. You had a great time and were in touch with your silliness and humor. That's wonderful. Your warmth really came through."

Then you suggest what needs work. Example: "I felt you were holding back on some of your impulses. Trust your intuition. You had an impulse when I suggested being a waiter, and you blocked it. I saw that you were thinking how you wanted to do it."

I often make suggestions to someone as to where to get help with specific areas that need work. If they're tense, I might suggest an African dance class. If they have a tight voice, I might suggest a speech class. Sometimes I'll tell them to do things where they just have fun and can be a kid again. There are many suggestions that I discuss with each person, depending on what I see in the exercise.

The amount of time you spend on *Song and Dance* depends on how many people volunteer to do the exercise. In a three-hour workshop, I usually have two or three volunteers. Then we spent the rest of the time on group improvisations. If you have a shorter or longer workshop, you can adjust the amount of time you spend on *Song and Dance* accordingly.

Having to play safe stunts any artist.
— Uta Hagen

Bringing Out Your Masculine/Feminine Parts
45-90 minutes

PURPOSE: Develops the ability to take risks
Increases the appreciation of gesture
Explores the ability to switch roles

Notes to the Leader

You might want to ask your group the following questions: Why would it be valuable to get in touch with your masculine parts if you're a woman? Why would it be valuable to get in touch with your feminine parts if you're a man?

Procedure

Find your own space in the room. Don't face anyone in the group. Close your eyes. Relax your body. Feel your breath flowing in and out. Slowly let your body transform to a man if you are a woman. If you are a man, let your body slowly transform to a woman. Start with your right hand. Feel your hand changing.

1. Do you wear rings?
2. What is the thickness of your fingers?
3. What are your fingernails like?
4. Go up your right arm. What does your arm feel like?
5. Go across your back and down the other arm.
6. What is your neck like?
7. Notice your face, jaw, cheeks, lip, eyes, hair and tongue.
8. Go down your chest. Do your have breasts? What are they like?
9. What does your waist feel like?
10. Do you have hips? How large or small?
11. What is your fanny like?
12. Your shoulders?
13. Go inside your body.
14. What do you feel like inside your body?
15. Put clothes on. What do you choose to wear?
16. What are the textures, colors and design of your clothes?
17. Create an autobiography.
18. What is your essence?

Move around the space with your new body. How do you feel?

Group Improvisation

You're all at a fashion show. I'll tap one person to be the moderator. You're models. Even if your character would never be a model, he or she is one now. What clothes are you wearing? How is your hair done? The moderator introduces each of you as you walk down the center aisle.

Group Improvisation

You're in a cave on a tour. I'll tap one person to be the tour guide. You have all been excited or scared to take this tour. Stay in character the whole time.

Group Improvisation

You're in a hotel lobby. You may choose to speak or be silent. Figure out why you're in the lobby. You may be waiting for someone, reading a book, or just hanging out. Whatever you choose to do is fine. Stay in character and challenge yourself to try something daring or exciting as the scene progresses.

Divide Into Pairs

Find a partner and do an emotion recall. An emotion recall is when you recall a specific time you felt a strong emotion- joy, sadness, anger and so on. Example: It might be a time you won a contest, bought a puppy, or saw a sunset. You recall the place or scene of the event. You see the colors, textures and recall the smells of the scene. If there are other people present, you try to recall them in as much detail as possible. As you recall a certain emotion, you begin to re-live the experience again. Share an incredible, powerful moment that you experienced, something positive, in your real life. Be the opposite sex as you share it. Each person will have five minutes to share the experience.

Divide Into Groups Of Three Or Four

Each group will have twenty minutes and create a three-minute scene. In the scene, you are playing the opposite sex. You must have the following things in your scene:

1. A place, or where you are
2. An objective, or what you need from the other person
3. An action, or what you are doing to get what you want from the other person.

Spend ten minutes structuring the scene and the rest of the time rehearsing it. I'll go to each group and answer any questions you may have.

The Presentation

Before each scene goes up, I would like you to do one last thing. Keep the same scene you have worked on. But I would like you to do the scene as YOURSELF, being your own sex first. Then you will do the scene again, as the opposite sex.

Feedback Session

What did you notice when you did the scene as yourself? How did the scene change when you played the opposite sex? What was it like being a man or woman? What did you like about it? What did you dislike about it? How best did you empathize with the opposite sex? What did you learn that you didn't know before?

Know you what it is to be a child? It is to be something very different from the man of to-day. It is to have a spirit yet streaming from the waters of baptism; it is to believe in love, to believe in loveliness, to believe in belief; it is to be so little that the elves can reach to whisper in your ear; it is to turn pumpkins into coaches, and mice into horses, lowness into loftiness, and nothing into everything, for each child has its fairy godmother in its own soul.

— Francis Thompson, poet

Angels can fly because they take themselves lightly.

— G.K. Chesterton, writer

Innocence Exercise
45-90 minutes

PURPOSE: Reclaiming childhood and times of purity and innocence
Inspires freedom with mind and body
Heightens vulnerability

TOOLS: Drawing Board
Two 18" x 24" sheets of newsprint paper
Markers, pens, crayons

Procedure

Remember a time of innocence as a child or adult. These times could be watching a sunrise, seeing a puppy being born, and so on.

This exercise was born when someone asked, "How do you play innocence? How do you get innocence back?" We, as adults, wish to recapture times of purity and innocence. This exercise helps us to be vulnerable, as we were when we were children.

1. This exercise is NOT therapy.
2. The exercise is for fun, craziness and zaniness.
3. Be gentle with yourself as we go through each part.
4. Remember that YOU ARE IN CHARGE of the guided imagery that we'll be doing together. If something unpleasant comes in, just put that thought or memory on a piece of chiffon and float it away. You choose what you want to work with in this exercise.

Notes to the Leader

This exercise can be powerful and draining for your group. Make sure you have enough time to process the exercise.

Procedure

As a group, let's define innocence. Let's write on the newsprint the words that come up for you when you think of innocence.

Notes to the Leader

You're setting the stage so that when you do the guided imagery, the group associates some of the words that they think of when defining innocence. Groups I have taught have defined innocence with these words: new, fresh, no expectation, happy time, open, vulnerable, trusting, faith, pure, positive, no one can hurt me now, animals, safe, belief, no past, freedom, involved, fearless, expectant, anticipation, omnipotent and carefree.

Procedure

Find a space and lie down. Relax your body. Close your eyes. Get in touch with your breath dropping in and going out. Let in any sounds you hear in the room or outside. Don't block anything out. Let it all in. Remember, you're in charge. If a memory comes back that you don't want to deal with, just float it away on a piece of chiffon. You are in charge.

Notes to the Leader

You are repeating what you said at the opening of this exercise. Your group needs to hear these directions twice.

Procedure

I'd like you to remember a time of innocence as a child or adult. Relive it. Be there. See it in detail. Use all of your senses- sight, taste, smell, touch and sound. What was it like? How did you feel? Come back to this space. Feel your hands, your face, stretch your body. Relax.

Divide Into Pairs

Find someone you don't know well in the group. Share your experiences with them. As you listen to your partner, empathize with them.

Notes to the Leader

Repeat this exercise a second and third time. Have them share with a different partner the second and third time.

Feedback Session

Let's make a circle. Anyone is free to share what the experience was like for you and any insights you had. What did you learn? What did you find out about yourself? What surprised you? Let's list on a large sheet of paper the qualities of innocence that you discovered.

Assignment

Do the Innocence Exercise on your own. Lie down and remember as many times of innocence as you can. Make notes after you remember these times. You can keep a journal of times of innocence. These memories will unlock wonderful doors and experiences.

Divide Into Groups Of Three Or Four

Each group will structure an improvisation. Each person will pick one quality of innocence that they want to bring into their body.

1. Structure an improvisation as a group and base your character on one quality of innocence. Each person will probably portray a different quality.

2. The improvisation should have the following:

   a) **An objective:** something that each person wants from someone else in the group.

   b) **An action:** how you are going to get what you want; an action is a verb.

   c) **An obstacle:** something that is in the way of what you want. Example: My objective is that I need you to loan me $200. My obstacle in asking you is that I just borrowed $100 from you a month ago and haven't paid it back yet.

   d) You will have 25 minutes to work on the improvisation. I will visit each group and see how you're doing.

Feedback Session

What was this like for you? How did it feel? What did you see when each group did their improvisation? What did you learn?

Man's mind stretched by a new idea never goes back to its original dimensions.
— Oliver Wendell Holmes, Sr., writer and physician

Finale

My dream in writing this book was that it would inspire your work with your groups in new and exciting ways. I hope the exercises and the Art of Group Leadership has opened doors for you into your own creativity, magnificence and ingenuity.

I would love to hear from you about how this work has changed the people you work with and perhaps in some way has changed your life, too.

Please contact me at **jeannie@center4creativity.org** with any feedback, questions and insights that you have had. This work is never-ending and *your process* is just as important as any of these words you have just read. Always remember, trusting the moment is the most valuable gift you can give yourself.

We shall not cease from exploration.
And the end of all our exploring
Will be to arrive where we started
And know the place for the first time.
— T. S. Eliot

Appendices

A. Suggestions for Improvisational Settings

B. Suggestions for Two-Person Improvisations

C. Suggestions for Improvisations for Three or More People

D. Suggestions for Character Professions for Improvisations

E. Suggestions for Autobiographical Questions for Characters

F. Time Requirements for Each Exercise

G. Structuring the Group Time

H. Thoughts for Combining Exercises

I. The Value of Improvisation

J. Glossary of Terms

K. Keeping a Journal

L. 26 Tips on Taking Care of Yourself as a Group Leader

M. Recommended Texts: Personal Growth Books

N. Recommended Texts: Theater Books

NOTE: In Appendix A-D, I suggest ideas for improvisational settings and characters, and give you ideas for two-person improvisations and improvisations you can do with three or more people in your group.

You, as the facilitator can brainstorm with your group improvisational settings and ideas for characters and improvisations. You can always divide your group into teams and let them come up with their own improvisations, characters and places. All they need is a *place, who they are*, and a *conflict.* Having them come up with ideas, empowers your group and they will understand improvisation on a whole different level.

The following ideas will help jump-start your imagination. The sky is the limit!

Everything should be made as simple as possible, but not simpler.

— Albert Einstein

Appendix A
Suggestions For Improvisational Settings

Antiques store
Aquarium
Amusement park
Airport
Art gallery
Bank
Beauty shop
Beach
Bus station
Bus
Boat
Barber shop
Campground
Cave
Children's museum
Circus
Discotheque
Dance
Deli
Drug store
Flower shop
Farm
Forest
Garden
Graveyard
Guesthouse
Hotel
Hardware store
Hospital

Ice cream parlor
Inn
Laundromat
Lake
Law office
Museum
Motor home
Movie theater
Motel
New Age food store
New Age bookstore
On the street
Opera
Pet store
Pizza parlor
Pool room
Plane
Saks 5th Avenue Department Store
School
Ship
Swimming pool
Town Hall
Theater
Restaurant
Train
Train station
Tree house
Waiting room
Zen center

You are unique, and if that is not fulfilled, then something has been lost.
— Martha Graham

Appendix B
Suggestions For Two-Person Improvisations

Note: Improvisations **always** require a conflict between the people in the improvisation.

Place: Hair salon
Who: Beautician and customer
Conflict: Customer wants hair a bit shorter and has an important date in one hour. The stylist wants to dye the customer's hair since that is the latest fad.

Place: A river
Who: Two friends
Conflict: One is trying to convince the other one that there is an alligator in the water. The other person is hot and wants to swim and cool off.

Place: Small airplane
Who: Pilot and passenger
Conflict: Once they are in the air, the pilot admits that she has no idea how to fly the plane. The passenger has an important meeting he must attend in thirty minutes.

Place: Dog grooming shop
Who: Groomer and client
Conflict: The groomer gave the dog the wrong haircut.

Place: Zen center
Who: Zen teacher and student
Conflict: The student disagrees with the teacher.

Place: Stage for a rehearsal
Who: Director and actor
Conflict: The director is trying to give the actor directions and the actor is resisting what the director wants.

Place: Garden
Who: Two people taking a walk
Conflict: They disagree on the type of trees and flowers that they are seeing.

Place: Bus
Who: Bus driver and rider
Conflict: The rider doesn't have the exact change, but has a very important appointment.

Place: Kitchen in elegant hotel
Who: Head chef and a cook
Conflict: The cook disagrees with what the chef wants to do to a recipe.

Place: Lobby of fancy apartment building
Who: Doorman and trainee to be doorman
Conflict: The trainee cannot understand clearly what his job is.

Teamwork is the ability to work together toward a common vision.
The ability to direct individual accomplishments toward organizational objectives.
It is the fuel that allows common people to attain uncommon results.
— Andrew Carnegie, industrialist

Appendix C
Suggestions for Improvisations for Three or More People

Place: TV show
Who: Five animal experts
Conflict: The host lets each expert talk for thirty seconds on his/her animal. The experts can use a real animal or make up the names of their animals i.e. Miss Blip is an expert on the haliklapida. As each expert talks, the others start to contradict her. The host must maintain a smooth running show, or she will lose her job. Chaos has always broken out on her shows and this is the host's last chance.

Place: Office switchboard in a prestigious law firm
Who: Four switchboard operators
Conflict: This is an old-fashioned switchboard with long cords. One of the women is new and puts her cords in the wrong sockets. The switchboard is a mess. The boss is returning from the lunch room and they have two minutes to straighten the board.

Place: Restaurant kitchen
Who: Five cooks
Conflict: They are about to serve the main dish for a dinner of two hundred people. Two of the cooks think they left out the main ingredient. The dish must be served in ten minutes.

Place: Hospital operating room
Who: Two doctors, one patient, one nurse, one orderly
Conflict: An operation is in progress. The doctors can't agree on the type of thread that should be used to sew up an incision. The patient isn't doing well and a decision must be made quickly. Each person in the room has an opinion on the subject.

Place: Bank
Who: Loan officer and a couple
Conflict: Couple disagrees on how much money they need to borrow.

Place: Orchestra rehearsal
Who: Conductor and two violinists
Conflict: They disagree on how to play the music.

Place: Shore of a river
Who: Three fishermen
Conflict: They can't agree on where they should be on the shore to catch the best fish.

Place: Dance studio
Who: Choreographer and two dancers
Conflict: One dancer can't do what the choreographer wants.

Place: College business class
Who: Professor and three students
Conflict: The students don't understand what the professor is teaching, and they must understand it in order to pass a test.

Play is the only way the highest intelligence of humankind can unfold.
— Joseph Chilton Pearce, author

Appendix D
Suggestions For Character Professions For Improvisations

This list includes over two hundred professions. It will give you ideas of which characters you might assign in the improvisations. It's also fun to let the people in your group pick the kind of character they would like to be. Feel free to assign characters that you feel will be challenging. Sometimes people need to stretch, and assigning them a challenging character accomplishes that task! This list is just the beginning.

Acting teacher
Actor
Actress
Administrator
Anchorperson
Animal trainer
Anthropologist
Appraiser
Army officer
Art historian
Artist
Art teacher
Astrologist
Astronaut
Athlete
Athletic trainer
Auctioneer
Baker
Ballroom dance teacher
Banjo player
Banker
Bank officer

Bank teller
Barber
Barmaid
Bartender
Basketball player
Baseball manager
Baseball player
Bass player
Beautician
Blacksmith
Bodyguard
Bookkeeper
Breeder of animals
Builder
Building inspector
Bum
Bus driver
Businessperson
Cabinetmaker
Calligrapher
Cameraman

Candle maker
Captain of a ship
Card shark
Career counselor
Car mechanic
Carpenter
Cartoonist
Cashier
Caterer
Cat groomer
Chauffeur
Chef
Choirmaster
Circus performer
Cleaning lady
Clown
Coach
College administrator
College teacher
Columnist
Cook

Composer
Computer programmer
Conductor
Congress person
Construction worker
Cosmetician
Dancer
Dance teacher
Detective
Disc jockey
Doctor
Dog groomer
Dog trainer
Doorman
Driving teacher
Drummer
Editor
Electrical engineer
Electrician
Electrologist
Elephant trainer
Elevator operator
English teacher
Factory worker
Farmer
Father
Fiddler
Film director
Fireman
Fisherman
Florist
Football player
Fortune teller

Gardener
Garbage collector
Geologist
Go-go dancer
Grave digger
Grandfather
Grandmother
Guitar player
Guru
Gynecologist
Hairdresser
Handwriting expert
Harmonica player
Harpsichordist
Headmaster/mistress
Historian
Hockey player
Hospital administrator
Hospital technician
Hotel manager
Innkeeper
Intern
Inventor
Janitor
Jeweler
Jockey
Judge
Lawyer
Legislator
Librarian
Lifeguard
Life insurance salesperson
Lighthouse keeper

Lion tamer
Lobbyist
Lumberjack
Mailman
Makeup artist
Maître d'
Maid
Manicurist
Map maker
Marine
Math teacher
Mechanic
Medicine man
Medium
Meteorologist
Meter maid
Military person
Minister
Model
Mother
Movie manager
Movie star
Museum curator
Musician
Nanny
Navy officer
New car salesperson
Newspaper reporter
Newscaster
Novelist
Nun
Nurse
Nursery school teacher

Opera singer
Optometrist
Orchestra conductor
Orderly
Painter
Pediatrician
Pet shop owner
Pharmacist
Philanthropist
Philosopher
Photographer
Pianist
Pilot
Playwright
Plumber
Poet
Policeman
Politician
President of the United States
Priest
Principal
Printer
Prison warden
Private investigator
Private school teacher
Producer
Psychiatrist
Psychic
Psychologist
Psychology teacher
Public school teacher
Publisher
Rabbi

Race car driver
Racketeer
Radio announcer
Radio technician
Realtor
Receptionist
Repairman
Rock star
Runner
Sailor
Salesperson
Seamstress
Secretary
Senator
Servant
Shoe salesman
Singer
Ski instructor
Social worker
Soda jerk
Soldier
Spinster
Sports car driver
Spy
Stage director
Stage manager
Steward
Stewardess
Stunt man
Stockbroker
Sunday school teacher
Surgeon
Surveyor

Swami
Tailor
Talk show host
Taxi cab driver
Teacher
Telephone operator
Telephone repairman
Therapist
Ticket taker
Toll taker
Tool and dye maker
Tour guide
Track star
Train conductor
Trapeze artist
Travel agent
Truck driver
Tutor
Upholsterer
Used car salesperson
Vet
Violinist
Waiter
Waitress
Watchmaker
Weaver
Window washer
Writer

The art of teaching is the art of assisting discovery.
— Mark Van Doren, Pulitzer Prize-winning poet

Appendix E
Suggestions for Autobiographical Questions for Characters

When you ask your group to create a character, ask them some of the following questions:

Where do you live?

What do you do for a living?

Do you live with others or alone?

Do you have friends/a best friend?

With what color glasses do you see the world?

What is your life view?

What is your most favorite thing to do in the whole world?

What don't you like to do?

Are you political?

What do you keep in your right-hand dresser drawer?

What really matters to you in life?

What are your values?

What do you do when you are alone?

If you had one million dollars, what would you do?

Do you do any sports/physical activities?

How do you dress?

Where do you like going on vacations?

What kind of house/apartment do you live in?

Do you live in a building or on the street?

What do you do with your free time?

Do you have pets?

What is your day like/a typical day?

How old are you?

Do you have family?

What does your body look like?

How do you feel about your body?

What do you consider your good points and bad points?

Feel free to make up your own questions to ask your group.

Time spent laughing is time spent with the gods.
— Japanese proverb

Appendix F
Time Requirements for Each Exercise

This list only applies if you do the *entire* exercise. The time requirements are based on the number of participants in the group. If you have more than twelve people in your group, some of the exercises might take longer. And sometimes it doesn't matter whether you have a group of twelve or twenty-five people or even fifty or one hundred people.

NOTE: These time requirements are general. Most of the exercises have many parts. You can take any part of an exercise and you'll have more than one hundred shorter exercises between fifteen and thirty minutes in length. However, some of these, such as *Elements: Air-Fire-Water-Earth*, were you to facilitate the entire exercise, could take several hours.

5-10 minutes
Energizing Series

10-15 minutes
Relaxation Series

15-30 minutes
Box Closing In
Drawing Exercise
Here and Now Exercise
Slow Motion
The Most Exciting Things

30-45 minutes
Animal Image
Closing Exercise
Concentration Exercise
Conditioning Forces

30-45 minutes (cont.)
Finding your Center
Listening Exercise
Mask Exercise
Musical Tune
My Name Is
Opening Exercise for Group
Three-Imitate-Three
Song and Dance

30-60 minutes
Color Exercise: Verbal
Color Exercise: Non-verbal
Fantasy and Dream
Float the Judges Away
Inanimate Quality
Movement Traits
Music Exercise
Object by the Bed
Panel of Experts
Pick a Voice
Poems

45-60 minutes
Emotion Memory Exercises
Nature
Newspaper Article
Painting Exercise
Panel of Experts
Picture Exercise
Person You Know Well
Sense Memory Exercises
Stereotypes
You as a Child, Teen, Twenties and Your Fantasy Exercise

45-90 minutes

Being Someone Opposite from You
Best Physical Part
Bringing Out Your Masculine/Feminine Parts
Delsarte Exercise
Innocence Exercise
Movement Qualities
Shape Exercise
Worst Physical Part

60-90 minutes

Elements: Air-Fire-Water-Earth
Object Exercise
Perfect People Party

It is the supreme art of the teacher to awaken joy in creative expression and knowledge.
— Albert Einstein

Appendix G
Structuring the Group Time

The exercises in this book were taught to many different groups with different time requirements. Many of my workshops were three hours in length and lasted for ten weeks. Other workshops lasted for a day and were six to eight hours in length. Many of the exercises were taught in a three-day retreat that started Friday evening and ended Sunday at 2 p.m.

In each workshop, whether a day-long or a three-hour workshop, I always divided the time in the following way.

1. Relaxation and warm-up time.

2. Time for questions.

3. Group work so everyone in the group had a chance to create and work together.

4. Individual time, working with partners on their own, or dividing the group into triads for group work that they would then show to the rest of the group.

5. Sometimes there were exercises where I was coaching individuals and the group watched.

The main rule that I always followed was that **everyone** in the group worked every single session. The exercises are participatory and experiential and it is important that everyone participate in every session.

For a three-hour class, I might have group work for the first half of the class and individual coaching for the second half of the class, or vice-versa.

The only real valuable thing is intuition.
— Albert Einstein

Appendix H
Thoughts for Combining Exercises

One friend asked me to include a recipe for combining the different exercises that would be like a menu in a cookbook. I tried to do this and realized that there is no formula for what exercises fit best with each other. There are hundreds of different combinations you can use.

You can take a part of one exercise and use it with a part of another exercise. The book contains over 120 shorter exercises between fifteen and thirty minutes in length. Let your intuition be your guide.

The one important thing I will suggest, is that if you are sitting for one exercise, it is wonderful to be moving for the next one, or vice-versa. Variety is the spice of life.

Here are some questions to think about when you structure your workshops and the exercises you'll be using that day.

- What objectives do you want to accomplish?
- What are the ages of your group?
- How long do you want your group sitting?
- How long do you want your group moving?
- Does the exercise feel light and whimsical to you?
- Do the exercises feel more serious and intense?
- What exercises can you do to warm up your group for your time together?
- What kind of rhythm would you like to have in the workshop?
- What is the overall feel that you want the workshop to have?
- What exercises can you choose that contrast with each other, so your group is exposed to a variety of colorful experiences?

The greater the obstacle, the more glory in overcoming it.
— Molière, French playwright (1622-1673)

Appendix I
The Value of Improvisation

In several workshops, I asked participants to write what they felt was the value of improvisation. Here are some of their wonderful responses:

It's a letting go of inhibitions.

It's a great lesson for listening to others.

It's so freeing.

Improv keeps me on my toes.

It helps me think quickly and therefore forces me to be in the moment.

It is a way to just be.

It is a connection with other actors.

It brings out my spontaneity.

It brings out our creativity.

Improvisation is about not judging anything.

It's about swinging between the trees.

You think on your feet.

It's great for taking risks.

It makes me smile.

Improvisation challenges every part of my being.

I get crazy and goofy.

It makes you feel so vulnerable and completely naked.

It creates a positive atmosphere.

Improv is fun stuff.

It breaks you out of a shell.

It's all about experimentation.

It forces you to be flexible and spontaneous.

There is no right and no wrong.

It's fun not knowing what is coming next.

It develops our imagination.

Improv helps the bonding.

It lets me hang loose and have fun.

I was so scared to do improv but now I love it and can really let myself go.

There are some truthful moments during improv.

I make new discoveries without my third eye bugging me.

It forces you to think quickly and act on impulse.

It forces you to listen to what others have to say, instead of just acting for yourself.

Improv is pure uncensored heart and mind.

It teaches you to trust your partner.

It is a wonderful tool for the exploration of freedom and being outside the box.

It can help us overcome our fears and other reservations of being in front of people.

It forces me to get rid of my inhibitions and that's why it is FABULOUS!

When one does not search for security, true creativity fills the space that might not have been opened otherwise.

It teaches you to just try things and not to worry about what other people think.

It forces you to pay close attention to the other person so you are not so worried about yourself.

What the teacher is, is more important than what he teaches.
— Karl Menninger, psychiatrist

Appendix J
Glossary Of Terms

Emotion And Sense Memory

On stage, if an actor must feel sad, he might think of a memory in his past where he felt sad. Example: The actor remembers when his mom was in the hospital and she looked fragile. The actor thinks of objects from the event to trigger the sadness i.e. her head on the white pillow, the look in her eyes, the smell of the room. And then the actor forgets the memory. He only uses the memory as a *springboard* to the scene. If he remembers the memory while he is doing the scene, then he's not in the moment of the scene, but in the moment of his emotion or sense memory. It's important that an actor doesn't think of the saddest thing that ever happened to him, because he would be lost in his emotion and forget about the scene or improvisation he is doing.

All emotion memories have sense memories associated with them—taste, smell, sound and touch. Sense memories arouse the senses and give the emotional memory pictorial and sensual details. Sense memory is the recall of physical sensations using one or more of your five senses. Example: You walk into the room and smell something burning. You can remember when you burnt a cake. In a scene, if you stroke a child's cheek and feel tender, you could remember stoking a baby's cheek.

Objectives And Actions

Objective: An objective is defined as what a person wants, needs and desires from another person. You ask, "What do I want from the other person?"

Action: The action is the HOW you get what you want. The HOW you get what you want reveals who you are as a person/character. Actions are verbs. Your action must make you 'hot' to go. The action is always directed at the other person. It is something you can physically DO to the other person. You pick one action to do. If that action doesn't get you your objective, you pick another action. The following are examples of objectives and actions. You can only play one action at a time. If one doesn't work, you try another action.

Objective: Jim wants Susan to go to the party with him.
Action: How does he get her to go with him: caress, tickle, embarrass, harass?

Objective: Jane wants to borrow twenty-five dollars from Mindy.
Action: How does she get the money she needs: tease, shake, stroke, hit?

Objective: John wants Annette to help him clean the apartment.
Action: How does he get Annette to help him: cajole, bribe, hug?

List Of Actions

abuse	harass	nick	shun	bulldoze	humiliate
adore	heal	nibble	shock	bury	frighten
aggravate	horrify	needle	stroke	calm	intoxicate
alarm	humiliate	nag	stun	captivate	infuriate
allure	hurt	nurture	tackle	charm	pester
amaze	hypnotize	nuzzle	stamp	cherish	needle
amuse	hammer	overpower	squash	claw	nibble
annihilate	hit	overwhelm	spew	consume	scorn
annoy	hug	pacify	swipe	crave	shelter
bait	gag	pamper	startle	cuddle	shrink
battle	gouge	pound	yank	deflate	shun
beg	infuriate	press	wrestle	degrade	sicken
calm	inspire	pet	worship	delight	smash
captivate	insult	poke	weaken	destroy	soften
caress	intimidate	puncture	twist	devastate	soothe
castrate	irritate	pull	trample	devour	romance
charm	jab	pop	trap	disgrace	pat
coddle	jeer	pulverize	torture	disembowel	scintillate
coax	jerk	pummel	tickle	disgust	slay
consume	impale	ravage	titillate	dominate	suffocate
crave	kick	ram	tap	drug	yank
crush	knife	rub	tease	drag	weaken
embarrass	lick	rip	terrorize	drill	wring
engulf	massage	rape	thrill	dupe	thrash
enrage	mesmerize	rock	thwart	eat	trample
entice	mock	rupture	taunt	elbow	spank
entertain	molest	push	tear	embrace	spin
expose	mother	slay	touch	enfold	squeeze
frisk	smother	scratch	torment	enrage	slaughter
flatter	mutilate	seduce	ambush	ensnare	suffocate
fondle	screw	split	applaud	envelop	wound
flagellate	sock	snap	attack	expose	woo
frighten	mount	scorch	bombard	inflame	whip
frustrate	menace	shove	bludgeon	stick	
grab	melt	shake	bump	jostle	

Obstacles

The objective is what you want from another person and the obstacle is in the way of your objective. An obstacle is something in the way of what you want. It's a roadblock. You ask: Who's against me? What's against me?

Uta Hagen, a famous actress and acting teacher told a story of a wonderful situation. She was in a play and her character was so happy, that she wanted to jump for joy. Her obstacle was gravity. She couldn't jump high enough and this made her try even harder to jump high.

Here's an example of an objective, action and obstacle from *Macbeth*. The scene is where Lady Macbeth tries to convince Macbeth to kill the King.

Lady Macbeth's objective: Convince Macbeth to kill the King

Action: Flatter him, insult him, seduce him

Her obstacle: Her fright at him doing the deed

Why do we use obstacles? *They make you work harder to get what you want.* Obstacles raise the stakes and make the improvisation more intense. It's interesting to see in your own life, times you have objectives, HOW you get what you want from another person and what obstacles are in your way. Here's another example of an objective and an obstacle.

I'm excited to teach my class and my objective is to excite the group about a new technique I am teaching. My obstacles are: My stomach hurts, there are three disruptive students, my boss is watching at the door and if I don't do a good job, I may lose my job and the room is too cold. Those are all obstacles that raise the stakes. My obstacles don't stop me from pursuing my objective, but they do make it harder for me to get what I want.

If you are alone, an objective may also be something you want to do for yourself and others. Example: You want to set a beautiful table. Here are some other examples of obstacles:

Character: I am a perfectionist and create tension because I must set it perfectly.

My past: My mother told me I never did it the correct way.

Time: The guests are arriving in five minutes.

Circumstances: My husband is asleep in the next room and I want to be quiet so I don't wake him up.

Relationship: Important people are coming to dinner and I want to impress them.

Place: The table is too small to fit everything that I want to put on the table.

Weather: It is cold outside and the heat in the house is broken.

Conditioning Forces

A conditioning force is a condition that influences your behavior, how you move, how you feel and how you communicate. It can affect your senses. Example: You are hard of hearing. You have clouded vision. You are hot because it is almost one hundred degrees.

A conditioning force affects what you are doing. Example: You are late, so you hurry. You have a sleeping child in the next room, so you must be quiet.

Creating An Ensemble

In theater, the director tries to create an ensemble with his/her cast. Creating an ensemble means working as a team which makes your cast cohesive. This inspires artistic and creative work, and bonds the people in the cast. If there is a warm and caring ensemble of actors, their work transforms and inspires both the cast and everyone in the theater. The same is true in your workshops. You want to create an ensemble, so members are supporting each other with warmth and care.

Increases Movement Vocabulary

When an actor studies theater, a movement teacher will stretch the actor to his limit and hopefully make the actor's body able to do many types of roles and characters. When an actor has a wide range in his movement vocabulary, he can use his body in many different ways. His creativity is enhanced and he discovers new ways he can use his body and voice.

Any actor wants the widest movement vocabulary possible so he is able to act in many types of plays doing a wide variety of roles. In your groups, you want to inspire and challenge your members in their creative growth.

I hear remarks in the street or in a shop and I retain them.
You must constantly observe: a walk, a limp, a run;
how a head inclines to one side when listening; the twitch of an eyebrow;
the hand that picks the nose when it thinks
no one is looking; the mustache puller; the eyes that never look at you;
the nose that sniffs long after the cold is gone.

— Laurence Olivier

Appendix K
Keeping a Journal

Keep a journal with observation assignments, feedback on the classes, questions and whatever else you choose to write. The journal can be written in a stream of consciousness, just thoughts, and with no punctuation.

Notes to the Leader

The journals are not to be corrected for spelling and punctuation. Whatever anyone writes in their journal is fine, as long as you can read it and it is legible.

If there's a page or pages that someone doesn't want you to read, ask that they fold those pages in half, and you won't read them.

PURPOSE

It's a good idea to share the purpose of the journals with your group. Ask how many of them keep journals and have them share why they like keeping one. Here are several reasons why a journal is valuable.

1. It's an outlet for feelings.
2. Things can be written in a journal that someone prefers to write about and not talk about. These thoughts can be private, just for themselves, or may be a note to the group leader that is easier to write about than share in person.
3. It can feel like a personal letter between the group member and leader.
4. Journals keep the leader in contact with each member of the group. Members may share something important going on in their lives.
5. It provides a structure for us to pay closer attention to our lives.
6. The journal acts as a reflector and can be looked at to see patterns in our lives.

7. We can reflect upon the meaning of significant events.
8. We become more aware of our self, the world, and other people.
9. It can be used as a values clarification tool.
10. We commit ourselves by keeping a journal.
11. Sometimes we don't even know what we may write. It just comes out and THEN we know how we feel about something or some issue.
12. We cannot write down all of our thoughts. We must choose the ones that are most important to us.
13. We can resolve problems through writing.
14. Useful associations and images begin to emerge in our journals.
15. Keeping a journal is an invaluable life-long process in creativity.
16. Writing is a catharsis and a letting go of steam. It is a venting tool.
17. We can write dreams, fantasies and visualizations.
18. We can see the patterns in our lives.

Notes to the Leader

Assign a journal assignment each week. You may choose to assign an observation and a personal assignment. Journals can be turned in every few weeks to the teacher.

Procedure

There will be two types of assignments for your journals. One is an observation assignment and one is personal assignment per week. Observation assignments will build your observational skills. You follow people, discreetly for twenty minutes and then write about what you saw when you get home.

For the observations, observe people you do NOT know. You will be following many different types of people. You may observe people while you sit in a restaurant, in a hotel lobby, in a train station or any place you go to do errands. If you follow them on the street, stay far away from them so you respect his space. Personal assignments can be written any time when you are peaceful and alone.

Following are some types of people you can observe. It's best to write in your journal soon after you do your observations.

Observations of People

Sad	Scared	Excited	Vulnerable	Mushy	Neighbor
Peaceful	Jittery	Independent	Strange	Effusive	Someone you see daily
Euphoric	Numb	Playboy	Hard	Tense	Cynical
Bored	Angry	Playgirl	Aggressive	Proud	Joyful

Irresponsible
Responsible
Conceited
Obnoxious
Frenetic
Very old
Pompous
Mushy
Hippie
Male chauvinist
Feminist
Hang loose
Formal
Rude
Truck driver
Hostile
Loving
Good mother
Good father
Aloof
Bouncy
Colorful
Ashamed
Cool
Organized
Uptight
Flaky
Unconventional
Flirt
With a negative self-image
With a positive self-image
No concentration
Not having a good time
Having a good time

Someone you'd like to be around
Someone you don't like to be around
Old country ethnic person
Strange walk
Strange voice
Laughter of a person
Person who is self-conscious
Laughter of a person who is too loud
Soft laughter
Two people loving their meal
Likes rock n' roll
Likes classical music
Defensive
Not too bright
Safe person
Ethnic person
Ages 6-10
Ages 11-16
Ages 17-21
Ages 22-29
Ages 30-40
Ages 41-50
Ages 51-60
Ages 61-70
Ages 71-80
Ages 81-90
Ages 91-100
Distracted
Numb
In physical pain
In psychological pain
Inner fury
Saintly
Automaton

Realized
Lazy
Supermarket cashier
Supermarket bagger
Yelled at
Yelling at
Romanced
The romancer
Ostracized
Stroked
Very thin
Very heavy
Burnt out
Very nervous
Scared
Doing a task
Waiting
Sitting
Administrator
Banker
Bitter
Traditional
Policeman
Policewoman
Meter maid
Personal caretaker
Sloppy
Smoker
Lonely
Dynamics at a party
Overhear two kids talking
Person doing a sport
Eating breakfast
Having an argument

Dominating parent & child
Elegant
Was different in younger days
Middle-aged who looks young and why
Middle-aged who looks old and why
Old who looks young and why
Old who looks old and why
Musician
Painter
Plumber
Gardener
Writer
Hostess
Person relaxing
Person stressed
Group of women/men in the 20's, 30's, 40's, 50's, 60's
Nun
Student
Beautician
Librarian
Train conductor
Husband and wife getting along
Husband and wife not getting along
Two lovers
Brother-sister
Friends
Person reminds you of an animal
Withdrawn
Super slow
In his/her own world
In a hurry
In an uncomfortable situation

Curious
Pushy
Professional and doesn't let you forget it
Warm
Loving
Great humility
Focused
Unfocused
Store owner
Beautiful and knows it
Beautiful and doesn't know it
Handsome and knows it
Handsome and doesn't know it
Dowdy
Happy wife and unhappy husband
Happy husband and unhappy wife
Unhappy couple
Naïve
Middle class
Upper class
Depressed
Positive energy person
Three walks
Three voices
Three different professions
Ethnic
Cartoon character
Three people waiting
Listen to the laughter of three people
Watch someone you admire
Profession you see daily but take for granted

Personal observations: These observations are about YOU. You're writing your own reflections and thoughts about the subject. Here are some personal observations you can assign.

Describe hearing something beautiful.
Describe tasting something beautiful.
Describe touching something wonderful.
Describe smelling something good.
Describe smelling something bad.
What do you have anxiety about and how are you dealing with it?
Write about the date one year from today and what your life is like.
Where will you be in five years? Ten years?
What are the four most important things to you in life?
If you could pick a time in history to live in, what would it be and why?
Eat a meal, pretending you are blind.
If you could open a shop, what would it be?
What would a perfect day be like?
What is your perfect environment?
Describe a fantasy day you would love.
Describe a fantasy hour you would love.
If you could meet anyone, living or dead, who would it be?
If someone were describing you, what would they say?
If you could take a trip anywhere, where would it be?
What is your greatest responsibility?
How could you travel lightly?
What is your essence?
What piece of music describes you the best?
What color describes you best?
What animal describes you best?
What inanimate object describes you best?
How old do you feel?
What means of transportation describes you and why?
If you were three pieces of fruit, what would you be?
What gives you more energy than you've ever had?
See yourself through the eyes of a dog in a park and describe what you see.

What environments do you thrive in?
What are your dreams?
Hug a tree and write about it.
Think of three times in your life when you were vulnerable.
Find yourself in a situation that causes a certain reaction in you.
What three things are you working on in your life?
Do an evening review of the highlights of your day.
Write about twenty-five things you are grateful for.
I need…
I don't need…
What does spirituality mean to you?
What weather describes you best?
What feeling did you have today that was powerful?
Describe a sad experience.
Find three times during the day when you talk to yourself.
What is the most important thing to you?
What ways could you change and be happier?
What ways could you change and be more peaceful?
If this were the last year of your life, what changes would you make in your relationships, your work life and family life?
What are the commitments in your life that matter to you?
Where are you experiencing resistance in your life?
What is your vision for your life?
What is your vision for the world?
What are the gifts you bring to the world?
What would you be like if you were completely authentic, free and passionate?
What experience in your life are you looking for?
What are your criteria for a great relationship?
How do you define authenticity?
How important is looking good to you?
List your ten best attributes.
To what people or ideas do you compare yourself?
What do you like best about yourself?
Take a risk in a primary relationship.

Take a risk at work.
Take a risk with a friend.
What is at stake when you are vulnerable with someone?
What does success mean to you?
When you are ninety years old and look back, what do you think will be most important to you?
What is your interpretation of risk?
What are the prices and rewards of risking?
When have you risked and it didn't work out?
When have you risked and succeeded?
What is important to you regarding family, work, health and relationships?
What situations are stressful to you?
What is your sense of adventure?
Describe an adventure you've had.
What adventures would you like to have?
What is your vision of the future?
What is missing or what do you need to accomplish this vision?
When do you feel joyful?
What things do you appreciate having in your life?
Remember three times you felt inner peace.
List three areas in which you allow yourself freedom.
List three new experiences or skills that you would like to learn.
What quantum leap would you like to take?
What is one area of your life that you would like to change?
What color glasses do you see the world with?
How do you express your sensuality?
Do you express your sensuality?
When you are sad, how do you get out of it?
What makes your day wonderful?
How do you stay centered?
Describe a snowstorm.
What interactions do you enjoy the most?
If you could be someone else, who would you be?
What are some skills you would like to develop?
What does creativity mean to you?

What are your dreams?

What gives you pain?

Describe your greatest joy?

Write a poem.

Go to a children's store and buy three dollars worth of fun.

How do you get out of a tight situation?

What do you do in your quiet time?

What do you need most in your life?

Who do you need most in your life?

How do you clutter your day?

What qualities does your best friend have?

What is one challenge you can set for yourself this week?

Describe a pencil in an interesting way.

Describe a pet you have or had.

What was the most exciting thing you have done?

What absolutely drives you crazy?

What was the saddest moment of your life?

What was the most challenging thing in your life?

What is the most challenging thing in your life right now?

What was the poignant memory you have?

What was the most thrilling memory of your life?

What was the most romantic time of your life?

What do you feel right now?

What are the highlights of your life?

What is your philosophy of life?

What are your priorities?

Write a love letter to yourself.

What is your dream house?

Where are you going in your life?

What gets you centered?

What is the most incredible conversation you have ever had?

Describe a time you felt lonely.

When was a time that you felt hurt?

When was a time that you felt scared?

If you were a piece of furniture, what would you be?
If you were a flower, what would you be?
Write all the emotions you go through in a day.
What makes you feel elegant?
What distractions could you cut from your life?
Keep a time management log for a week. Write down everything you do in one day.
Write a thought for a day.
Describe a peaceful place you love.
What color describes you best?

To keep a lamp burning we have to keep putting oil in it.
— Mother Teresa

Appendix L
26 Tips for Taking Care of Yourself as a Group Leader

Journal: Keep your own personal journal of dreams, desires, priorities, reflections, hopes, needs, decisions, ideas, insights, anxieties and anything else that feels important to you. Journaling clears the air. It's a wonderful tool to clarify what you're feeling.

Personal Growth: Get fed by taking classes and workshops where you'll be challenged to take risks and grow.

Friends: Pick healthy people to have around you. Caring friends can give you valuable feedback and stimulate your growth.

Food: Eat healthy foods, which nurture and nourish you.

Gifts: Give yourself gifts. Do things that feed your soul.

Play: Find areas of your life where you can play. Playing releases your creative juices and gives you a change of pace.

Time Alone: Make sure that you have enough personal time for reflection and/or meditation.

Simplify: Clear away the things in your life that you don't need. Learn to travel lightly. This helps you stay focused and clear.

Do Things That Bring You Home: Find the constants and stabilities of your life, the things which give you the most pleasure and peace.

Exercise: Find a FUN way to stay in shape and stay healthy. Your mental state will be enhanced when you take care of your body.

Stimulation: You need stimulation for your mind, body and soul. Reading, meeting new people, talking with friends, traveling and writing help you create new and exciting experiences.

Relaxation: Find a type of relaxation where you can totally escape. Have "hang out" days where you have NO planned agenda.

Underwhelming Yourself: I took a workshop many years ago where we made a list of ways to underwhelm ourselves. Some things on the list were swimming, dancing, putting away your appointment book, taking a shower, doing things which you love to do. Make your own list of how you could underwhelm yourself.

Find That Special Place: Find a comforting place to go several times a week. It will be your 'island in the stream' to rest and refresh.

Your Home Environment: Make your home a warm and cozy place, a place you LOVE to be. Decorate your space with things you love to have around you.

Treat Yourself With Your Senses: Eat lovely meals, see great movies, and get a massage. Feed your senses in delicious ways. Fill your life with beauty.

Be Aware Of Your Time Clock: When do you work best? When do you play best? How much sleep do you need? Be aware of your time needs and life will flow more easily.

Find Role Models: Find people you admire and respect. Their way of being rubs off on you.

Boundaries: Setting boundaries with friends, family and colleagues. Saying "No" to someone else is saying "YES" to you.

Don't Procrastinate: Procrastination causes anxiety. A friend once said to me when I was procrastinating on a decision I had to make, "Make a decision, any decision, and you'll feel better." Procrastination uses energy needlessly.

Stay On Top Of Things: Stay in touch with your feelings. If there is a snag in your life, resolve it as quickly as possible. Know when to ask for help.

Peace, Challenges, Friendship, Love: These are the four things I need most in my life. What do you need most in your life?

Variety Is The Spice Of Life: Find many avenues of expression. Create new options and ways to grow.

Make A Book Of Seed Thoughts: Find quotes and thoughts that inspire you. Keeping them in one book is wonderful because you can refer to them when you need a pick-me-up or feel the need for inspiration.

Be In The Now: Try to lose expectations, of others and of yourself. Being in the now is like riding a wave of pure ecstasy.

Laugh: Find friends whom you love being with and whom you can laugh with. Laughter is one of the best ways in the world to take care of yourself.

You must draw first from the well to nourish and give to yourself.
Then there will be more than enough to nourish others.

— The Book of Runes

Appendix M
Recommended Texts: Personal Growth Books

Abbott, Winston O. *Letters from Chickadee Hill.* South Windsor, CT: Inspiration House, 1978.

_____. *Come Walk Among the Stars.* South Windsor, CT: Inspiration House, 1966.

_____. *Sing With the Wind.* South Windsor, CT: Inspiration House, 1968.

_____. *Have You Heard the Cricket Sing,* South Windsor, CT: Inspiration House, 1971.

_____. *Come Climb My Hill,* South Windsor, CT: Inspiration House, 1973.

Adams, Patch, MD. *Gesundheit!: Bringing Good Health to You, the Medical System and Society through Physical Service, Complementary Therapies, Humor and Joy.* Rochester, New York: Healing Arts Press, 1993.

Albom, Mitch. *Tuesdays with Morrie.* New York: Doubleday, 1997.

Amory, Cleveland. *The Cat and the Curmudgeon.* Boston: Back Bay Books, 2002.

_____. *The Best Cat Ever.* Boston: Back Bay Books, 2002.

_____. *Ranch of Dreams: A lifelong Protector of Animals Shares the Story of an Extraordinary Sanctuary.* New York: Viking, 1997.

Anderson, Joan. *A Year by the Sea.* New York: Broadway Books, 1999.

_____. *A Walk on the Beach.* New York: Broadway Books, 2004.

Arrien, Angeles. *The Second Half of Life.* Boulder, CO: Sounds True, 2005.

Assagioli, Roberto. *Act of Will.* New York: Penguin Books, 1971.

_____. *Psychosynthesis.* New York: Penguin Books, 1965.

Assaraf, John. *The Vision Board Book: How to Use the Power of Intention and Visualization to Manifest the Life of Your Dreams.* Hillsboro, OR: Beyond Words, 2008.

Attenborough, Richard. *The Words of Gandhi.* New York: Newmarket Press, 1982.

Barasch, Marc Ian. *Field Notes on the Compassionate Life: A Search for the Soul of Kindness.* Emmaus, PA: Rodale Books, 2005.

Ban Breathnach, Sarah. *Moving On.* Des Moines: Meredith Books, 2006.

_____. *Simple Abundance: A Daybook of Comfort and Joy,* NY: Warner Books, 1995.

Basso, Robert. *555 Ways to Put More Fun in Your Life.* Guildford, CT: Globe Pequot Press, 1994.

Bauman, Beau. *The Most Important Thing I've Learned in Life: 370 Lessons to Live By.* New York: Simon and Schuster, 1994.

Becker, Suzy. *All I Need to Know I Learned from My Cat.* New York: Workman Publishing, 1990.

Bender, Sue. *Plain and Simple: A Woman's Journey to the Amish.* New York: HarperOne, 1991.

_____. *Everyday Sacred: A Woman's Journey Home.* New York: HarperOne, 1996.

Benson, Herbert, M.D. *The Relaxation Response.* New York: Avon Books, 1975.

_____. *Beyond the Relaxation Response.* New York: Berkley Books, 1984.

_____. *Your Maximum Mind.* New York: Avon Books, 1987.

Berg, Yehuda. *The Power of Kabbalah.* Los Angeles: Kabbalah Centre International, 2004.

Berg, Karen. *God Wears Lipstick.* Los Angeles: Kabbalah Centre International, 2005.

Blatner, Adam (ed.). *Interactive and Improvisational Drama: Varieties of Applied Theatre and Performance.* Omaha: iUniverse, 2007.

Blum, Ralph. *A Book of Runes.* New York: St. Martins Press, 1982.

Bode, Richard. *First You Have to Row a Little Boat.* New York: Warner Books, 1993.

Bolles, Richard Nelson. *What Color is Your Parachute? 2011: A Practical Manual for Job-Hunters and Career-Changers.* Berkeley: Ten Speed Press, 2010.

Boone, J. Allen. *Kinship with All Life.* New York: HarperCollins, 1976.

Boorstein, Sylvia. *It's Easier Than You Think: The Buddhist Way to Happiness.* San Francisco: HarperOne, 1997.

_____. *Happiness Is an Inside Job.* New York: Ballentine Books, 2007.

Brown, H. Jackson. *A Father's Book of Wisdom.* Nashville: Rutledge Hill Press, 1988.

_____. *P.S. I Love You.* Nashville: Rutledge Hill Press, 1990.

Brown, Richard W. *The Soul of Vermont.* Woodstock, VT: The Countryman Press, 2001.

Brown, Jr. Tom. *Awakening Spirits: A Native American Path to Inner Peace, Healing and Spiritual Growth.* New York: Berkley Books, 1994.

_____. *The Search: The Continuing Story of The Tracker.* New York: Berkley Books, 1980.

_____. *The Vision: The Dramatic True Story of One Man's Search for Enlightenment.* New York: Berkley Books, 1988.

_____. *Grandfather: A Native American's lifelong search for truth and harmony with nature.* New York: Berkley Books, 1993.

Brussat, Frederick. *100 Ways to Keep Your Soul Alive: Living Deeply and Fully Every Day.* New York: HarperOne, 1994.

Buscaglia, Leo F. *The Fall of Freddie the Leaf: A Story of Life for All Ages.* Thorofare, NJ: Slack Inc., 1982.

_____. *Born for Love: Reflections on Loving.* New York: Ballantine Books, 1994.

Cameron, Julia. *The Artist's Way: A Spiritual Path to Higher Creativity,* New York: Tarcher, 2002.

_____. *Finding Water: The Art of Perseverance.* New York: Tarcher, 2009.

Camp, Joe. *The Soul of a Horse: Life Lessons from the Herd.* New York: Harmony Books, 2008.

Carey, Ken. *Flat Rock Journal: A Day in the Ozark Mountains.* San Francisco: Harper San Francisco, 1995.

Castaneda, Carlos. *A Separate Reality*. New York: Pocket Books, 1971.

Chase, Mildred Portney. *Just Being at the Piano*. Berkeley: Creative Arts Books, 1985.

Chetanananda, Swami. *The Breath of God*. Cambridge: Rudra Press, 1988.

Choquette, Sonia. *Your Heart's Desire: Instructions for Creating the Life You Really Want*. New York: Three Rivers Press, 1997

Choudhury, Bikram. *Bikram Yoga*. New York: HarperCollins. 2007.

Cleary, Thomas (ed.). *Zen Essence*. Boston: Shambhala, 1989.

Cohen, Andrea Joy. *A Blessing In Disguise: 39 Life Lessons from Today's Greatest Teachers*. New York: Berkley Books, 2008.

Cousins, Norman. *Anatomy of an Illness*. New York: Bantam Books, 1979.

Covey, Stephen R. *The 7 Habits of Highly Effective People*. New York: Fireside Books, 1989.

Crystal, John C. *Where Do I Go from Here with My Life?* Berkeley: Ten Speed Press, 1983.

Daley, Yvonne. *Vermont Writers: A State of Mind*. Lebanon, New Hampshire: University Press, 2005.

Dass, Ram. *The Only Dance There Is*. Garden City, NY: Anchor Books, 1974.

_____. *Grist for the Mill*. Santa Cruz: Unity Press, 1977.

_____. *Be Here Now*. New York: Crown Publishing, 1977.

_____. *Journey of Awakening: A Mediator's Handbook*. New York, Bantam Books, 1978.

_____. *Still Here*. New York: Riverhead Books, 2000.

Dass, Ram and Bush, Mirabai. *Compassion in Action: Setting Out on the Path of Service*. New York: Bell Tower, 1992.

Dean, Laura. *A Year on Monhegan Island*. New York: Houghton Mifflin, 1995.

Durrell, Gerald. *My Family and Other Animals*. New York: Penguin Books, 1984.

Desai, Yogi Amrit. *Happiness is Now*. Lenox, MA: Kripalu Communications, 1982.

_____. *Journal of the Spirit*. Lenox, MA: Kripalu Communications, 1985.

Dillard, Annie. *The Writing Life*. New York: Harper-Perennial, 1989.

Dobisz, Jane. *One Hundred Days of Solitude*. Boston: Wisdom Publications, 2008.

Dye, Dan. Beckloff, Mark. *Amazing Gracie: A Dog's Tale*. New York: Workman Publishing, 2000.

Dyer, Wayne. *Inspiration- Your Ultimate Calling*. New York: Random House, 2005.

Edelman, Marion Wright. *The Measure of Our Successes: A Letter to My Children and Yours*. Boston: Beacon Press, 1992.

Editors. *Random Acts of Kindness*. Berkeley: Conari Press, 1994.

_____. *More Random Acts of Kindness*. Newburyport, MA: Red Wheel/Weiser, 2007.

Eknath Easwaron. *Take Your Time: How to Find Patience, Peace and Meaning*. Tomales, CA: Nilgiri Press, 2006.

Emoto, Masaru. *The Hidden Messages in Water*. Hillsboro: Beyond Words Publishing, 2001.

Ferrucci, Piero. *What We May Be: Techniques for Psychological and Spiritual Growth.* Los Angeles: Jeremy P. Tarcher, 1982.

_____. *Inevitable Grace.* Los Angeles: Jeremy P. Tarcher, 1990.

_____. *The Power of Kindness: The Unexpected Benefits of Leading a Compassionate Life.* New York: Penguin Group, 2006.

Forward, Susan, Dr. *Toxic Parents.* New York: Bantam Books, 1989.

Franck, Frederick. *The Zen of Seeing.* New York: Vintage Books, 1973.

Frankl, Viktor. *Man's Search for Meaning.* New York: Washington Square Press, 1963.

Fromm, Erich. *The Art of Loving.* New York: Perennial Library, 1956.

Fulghum, Robert. *All I Really Need to Know, I Learned in Kindergarten.* New York: Ballantine Books, 1986.

Gallway, W. Timothy. *The Inner Game of Tennis.* New York, Bantam Books, 1979.

Gandhi. *The Words of Gandhi: Selected by Richard Attenborough.* New York: Newmarket Press, 1982.

Gellert, Michael. *The Way of the Small: Why Less is Truly More.* Lake Worth, FL: Nicolas-Hays, 2007.

Gethers, Peter. *The Cat Who Went to Paris.* New York: Ballentine Books, 1991.

_____. *A Cat Abroad.* New York: Ballantine Books, 1993.

_____. *The Cat Who'll Live Forever.* New York: Broadway Books, 2001.

Gibran, Kahlil. *The Prophet.* New York: Alfred A. Knoff, 1923.

Goldberg, Natalie. *Writing Down the Bones.* Boston: Shambhala, 1986.

_____. *Wild Mind.* New York: Bantam Books, 1990.

Goldstein, Joseph. *A Heart Full of Peace.* Boston: Wisdom Publications, 2007.

Goleman, Daniel, Kaufman, Paul and Ray, Michael. *The Creative Spirit.* New York: Penguin Books, 1992.

Gordon, Joann. *Be Happy at Work: 100 Women Who Love Their Jobs and Why.* New York: Random House, 2005.

Grandin, Temple and Johnson, Catherine. *Animals in Translation.* New York: Scribner, 2005.

_____. *Animals Make Us Human: Creating the Best Life for Animals.* Boston: Houghton Mifflin, 2009.

Gray, John Harvey and Lourdes. *Hand to Hand: The Longest-Practicing Reiki Master Tells His Story.* 2002.

Guilmartin, Nance. *Healing Conversations: What to Say When You Don't Know What To Say.* San Francisco: Jossey-Bass, 2002.

Gurney, Carol. *The Language of Animals: 7 Steps to Communicating with Animals.* New York: Random House, 2001.

Hall, Stacey and Brogniez, Jan. *Attracting Perfect Customers: The Power of Strategic Synchronicity.* San Francisco: Berrett-Koehler Publishers, Inc., 2001.

Hanh, Thich Nhat. *The Miracle of Mindfulness.* Boston: Beacon Press, 1975.

_____. *Being Peace.* Berkeley: Parallax Press, 1987.

_____. *The Heart of Understanding.* Berkeley: Parallax Press, 1988.

_____. *Present Moment Wonderful Moment*. Berkeley: Parallax Press, 1990.

_____. *Peace Is Every Step*. New York: Bantam Books, 1991.

_____. *Teachings on Love*. Berkeley: Parallax Press, 2007.

Hay, Louise L., *You Can Heal Your Life*. Carlsbad, CA: Hay House, 1984, 2004.

Hayward, Susan. *Begin It Now: A Guide for the Advanced Soul*. Crows Nest, Australia: In-Tune Books, 1987.

_____. *A Guide for the Advanced Soul*. Boston: Little Brown and Company, 1984.

Hendricks, Gay. *Five Wishes: How Answering One Simple Question Can Make Your Dreams Come True*. Novato, CA: New World Library, 2007.

Herrigel, Eugene. *Zen in the Art of Archery*. New York: Vintage Books, 1971.

Hicks, Esther and Jerry. *Ask and It Is Given: Learning to Manifest Your Desires*. Carlsbad, CA: Hay House, 2004.

_____. *The Law of Attraction*. Hay House, Carlsbad, CA, 2006.

_____. *Money, and the Law of Attraction: Learning to Attract Wealth, Health, and Happiness*. Carlsbad, CA: Hay House, 2008.

Hill, Ralph N. Hoyt, Murray, Hard, Jr. Walter R. *Vermont: A Special World*. Montpelier, VT: Vermont Life Magazine, 1983

Holzer, Burghild Nina. *A Walk Between Heaven and Earth: A Personal Journey on Writing and the Creative Process*. New York: Crown Publishers, 1994.

Housden, Roger. *Seven Sins for a Life Worth Living*. New York: Harmony Books, 2005.

Huxley, Laura. *You Are Not the Target*. Emeryville, CA: Marlowe & Company, 1998.

_____. *Between Heaven and Earth: Recipes for Living and Loving*. Santa Monica: Hay House, 1975.

Ingerman, Sandra. *Shamanic Journeying: A Beginner's Guide*. Boulder: Sounds True, 2004.

Izzo, John. *The Five Secrets You Must Discover Before You Die*. San Francisco: Berrett-Koehler Publishers, 2008.

Jacobs, Ruth Harriet, Ph.D. *Be An Outrageous Older Woman*. New York: HarperCollins Books, 1997.

James, Jennifer. *Success is the Quality of Your Journey*. New York: Newmarket Press, 1983.

_____. *Windows*. New York: Newmarket Press, 1987.

Jampolsky, Gerald, M.D. *Children as Teachers of Peace*. Millbrae, CA: Celestial Arts, 1982.

_____. *Love is Letting Go of Fear*. Millbrae, CA: Celestial Arts, 1979.

_____. *Teach Only Love*. New York: Bantam Books, 1983.

Jennison, Keith. *Vermont is Where You Find It*. Woodstock, VT: The Countryman Press, 1954.

Katie, Byron. *A Thousand Names for Joy*. New York: Harmony Books, 2007.

_____. *Loving What Is*. New York: Three Rivers Press, 2002.

Katz. Jon. *Izzy & Lenore: Two Dogs, an Unexpected Journey and Me*. New York: Villard Press, 2008.

Kaufman, Barry Neil. *Happiness is a Choice*. New York: Ballentine, 1994.

Kerasote, Ted. *Merle's Door: Lessons from a Freethinking Dog*. Orlando: Mariner Books, 2008.

Keyes, Ken. *Handbook to Higher Consciousness*. Berkeley: Living Love Center, 1972.

Kingston, Karen. *Clear Your Clutter with Feng Shui: Free Yourself from Physical, Mental, Emotional and Spiritual Clutter Forever*. New York: Broadway Books, 1999.

Kinkade, Amelia. *Straight from the Horse's Mouth: How to Talk to Animals and Get Answers*. New York: Crown Publishers, 2001.

_____. *The Language of Miracles*. Novato, CA: New World Library, 2006.

Krishnamurti, J. *Freedom from the Known*. New York: Harper and Row, 1969.

Kornfield, Jack. *Buddha's Little Instruction Book*. New York: Bantam Books, 1994.

Kubler-Ross, Elizabeth. *Questions of Death and Dying*. New York: Macmillan Publishing Company, 1974.

_____. *To Live Until We Say Goodbye*. Englewood Cliffs, NJ: Prentice-Hall, 1978.

Kushner, Harold. *When All You've Ever Wanted Isn't Enough*. New York: Summit Book, 1965.

_____. *When Bad Things Happen to Good People*. New York: Avon Books, 1983.

_____. *Who Needs God*. New York: Pocket Books, 1991.

LaBastille, Anne. *Woodswoman II*, New York: WW Norton & Co., 1987.

Lama Surya Das. *Letting Go of the Person You Used to Be: Lessons on Change, Loss and Spiritual Transformation*. New York: Broadway Books, 2004.

_____. *Awakening the Buddha Within*. New York: Broadway Books, 1997.

Lamont, Anne. *Bird by Bird; Some Instructions on Writing and Life*. New York: Pantheon Books, 1994.

Lange, Willem. *Tales from the Edge of the Woods*. Hanover, NH: University Press, 1998.

Lawler, Anthony. *The Temple in the House: Finding the Sacred in Everyday Architecture*. New York: Tarcher, 1994.

Hoblitzelle, Olivia Ames. *The Majesty of Your Loving: A Couple's Journey Through Alzheimer's*. Cambridge: Green Mountain Books, 2008.

LeClaire, Anne D. *Listening Below the Noise: A Meditation on the Practice of Silence*. New York: HarperCollins, 2009.

Lerner, Helene and Elins, Roberta. *Stress Breakers*. Minneapolis: Comp Care, 1985.

Levine, Stephen. *A Gradual Awakening*. Garden City, NY: Anchor Press, 1984.

_____. *Meetings at the Edge*. Garden City, NY: Anchor Press, 1984.

_____. *Who Dies*. Garden City, NY: Anchor Press, 1989.

Lindbergh, Anne Morrow. *Gift from the Sea*. New York: Vintage Books, 1978.

Lustbader, Wendy. *What's Worth Knowing*. New York: Jeremy Tarcher, 2004

Madson, Patricia Ryan. *Improv Wisdom: Don't Prepare, Just Show Up*. New York: Bell Tower, 2005.

May, Rollo. *Love and Will*. New York: Dell, 1974.

McMeekin, Gail. *12 Secrets of Highly Creative Women*. Newburyport, MA: Conari Press, 2000.

Middleton-Mox and Dwinell, Lorie. *After the Tears*. Deerfield Beach, Fl: Health Communications, 1986.

Miller, Peter. *Vermont People*. Waterbury, VT, 1990.

Mitchell, Stephen. *Tai Te Ching (translation)*. New York: Harper and Row, 1988.

Montgomery, Sy. *The Good Good Pig*. New York: Random House, 2006.

Moore, Thomas. Soul Mates: *Honoring the Mysteries of Love and Relationships*. Harper Collins Publishers, 1994.

_____. *A Life at work: The Joy of Discovering What You Were Born To Do*. New York: Broadway Books, 2008.

Moustakas, Clark. *Finding Yourself: Finding Others*. Englewood Cliffs, NJ: Prentice Hall, 1974.

Muktananda, Swami. *Where Are You Going? A Guide to the Spiritual Journey*. South Fallsburg, NY: Siddha Yoga Publications, 1994.

Nearing, Helen. *Loving and Leaving the Good Life*. Post Mills, VT: Chelsea Green, 1992.

Nerburn, Kent. *Small Graces: The Quiet Gifts of Everyday Life*. Novato, CA: New World Library, 1998.

_____. *The Hidden Beauty of Everyday Life*. Novato, CA: New World Library, 2006.

Niven, Dr. David. *100 Simple Secrets Why Dogs Make Us Happy*, New York: Harper Collins, 2007.

Paull, Candy. *The Art of Simplicity*. New York: Stewart, Tabori and Chang, 2006.

Pausch, Randy. *The Last Lecture*. New York: Hyperion Books, 2008.

Pearce, Herb. *The Power of the Enneagram*. New York: Penguin Group, 2007.

Pincott, J. (ed) *Success: Advice for Achieving Your Goals from Remarkably Accomplished People*. New York: Random House, 2005.

Pink, Daniel. *A Whole New Mind: Why Right-Brainers will Rule the Future*. New York: Riverhead Books, 2006.

Plasker, Dr. Eric. *The 100 Year Lifestyle*. Avon, MA: Adams Media, 2007.

Popov, Linda Kavelin. *A Pace of Grace: The Virtues of a Sustainable Life*. New York: Penguin Group, 2004.

Prather, Hugh. *Notes to Myself*. Moab, Utah: Real People Press, 1970.

_____. *I Touch the Earth, The Earth Touches Me*. Garden City, NY: Doubleday and Company, 1972.

_____. *Notes on Love and Courage*. Garden City, NY: Doubleday and Company, 1977.

_____. *There is a Place Where You Are Not Alone*. Garden City, NY: Doubleday and Company, 1980.

_____. *A Book of Games: A Course in Spiritual Play*. Garden City, NY: Doubleday and Company, 1981.

_____. *The Quiet Answer*. Garden City, NY: Doubleday and Company, 1982.

Rashid, Mark. *Horses Never Lie: The Heart of Passive Leadership*. Boulder: Johnson Books, 2000.

Richards, I. A. *Centering*. Middletown, CT: Wesleyan University Press, 1989.

Rilke, Rainer Maria. *Letters to a Young Poet*. New York: W.W. Norton and Company, 1934.

Robbins, Anthony. *Awaken the Giant Within: How to Take Immediate Control of Your Mental, Emotional, Physical and Financial Destiny.* New York: Simon and Schuster, 1991.

_____. *Unlimited Power.* New York: Ballantine Books, 1986.

_____. *Notes from a Friend: A Quick and Simple Guide to Taking Charge of Your Life.* New York: Simon and Schuster, 1995.

Robbins, John and Mortifee, Ann. *In Search of Balance.* Tiburon, CA: H. J. Kramer, 1991.

Rodegast and Stanton, Judith. *Emmanuel's Book.* New York: Bantam Books, 1985.

Rogers, Carl and Stevens, Barry. *Person to Person.* Moab, Utah: Real People Press, 1967.

Roger, John and McWilliams, Peter. *You Can't Afford the Luxury of a Negative Thought.* Los Angeles: Prelude Press, 1988.

Roman, Sanaya. *Living with Joy.* Tiburon, CA: HJ Kramer, 1986.

_____. *Personal Power Through Awareness.* Tiburon, CA: HJ Kramer, 1986.

_____. *Spiritual Growth.* Tiburon, CA: HJ Kramer, 1990.

_____. *Creating Money: Attracting Abundance.* Tiburon, CA. HJ Kramer/New World Library, 2007.

Rood, Ronald. *How Do You Spank a Porcupine?* Shelburne, VT: The New England Press, 1969.

Russell, Jerry and Renny. *On the Loose.* San Francisco: Sierra Club, 1967.

Salzberg, Sharon. *Lovingkindness: The Revolutionary Art of Happiness.* Boston: Shambhala, 2004.

_____. *Faith: Trusting Your Own Deepest Experience.* New York, Riverhead Books, 2003.

Sarton, May. *At Seventy.* New York: WW Norton, 1993.

Sark. *A Creative Companion: How to Free Your Creative Spirit.* Berkeley: Celestial Arts, 1989.

_____. *Inspiration Sandwich: Stories to Inspire Our Creative Freedom.* Berkeley: Celestial Arts, 1992.

Sher, Barbara. *I Could Do Anything If I Only Knew What It Was: How to Discover What You Really Want and How to Get It.* New York: Dell Publishing, 1994.

Shimoff, Marci. *Happy for No Reason: 7 Steps to Being Happy From the Inside Out.* New York: Simon and Schuster, 2008.

Siegel, Bernie, M.D. *Love, Medicine and Miracles.* New York: Harper and Row, 1986.

_____. *Peace, Love and Healing.* New York: Harper and Row, 1989.

_____. *How to Live Between Office Visits: A Guide to Life, Love and Health.* New York: Harper Collins, 1993.

_____. *Meditations for Everyday Living/Healing Meditations* (cassette tapes). New Haven: ECaP

Silverstein, Shel. *The Giving Tree.* New York: Harper and Row, 1964.

Simon, David. *The Ten Commitments: Translating Good Intentions into Great Choices.* Deerfield, FL: Health Communications, 2006.

Simon, Sidney. *Values Clarification.* New York: Hart Publishing Company, 1972.

Sinetar, Marsha. *Ordinary People as Monks and Mystics: Lifestyles of Self-discovery*. New York: Paulist Press, 1986.

_____. *Elegant Choices, Healing Choices*. New York: Paulist Press, 1988.

Smith, Penelope. *Animal Talk*. Tulsa: Council Oak Books, 1982, 1999.

_____. *When Animals Speak*. Hillsboro, OR: Beyond Words Publishing, 1999.

_____. *Animals in Spirit*. Hillsboro, Oregon: Beyond Words Publishing, 2008.

Stevens, Barry. *Don't Push the River*. Moab, Utah: Real People Press, 1970.

Stoddard, Alexandra. *Grace Notes: A Book of Daily Meditations, Thoughts & Inspirations for a Beautiful Life*. New York: HarperCollins, 1993.

Stoll, Jerry and Connel, Evan S. *I am a Lover*. Menlo Park: Pacific Coast Publishers, 1961.

Suzuki, Shunryu. *Zen Mind, Beginner's Mind*. New York: John Weatherhill, 1970.

Taylor, Terry Lynn. *Messengers of Light: The Angels' Guide to Spiritual Growth*. Tiburon, CA: HJ Kramer, 1990.

Tellington-Jones, Linda. *The Tellington TTouch: A Revolutionary Natural Method to Train and Care for Your Favorite Animal*. New York: Penguin Books, 1993.

Thakar, Vimala. *The Eloquence of Living*. San Rafael, CA: New World Library, 1989.

Tharp, Twyla. *The Creative Habit: Learn it and use it for Life*. New York: Simon & Schuster, 2006.

Tolle, Eckhart. *A New Earth: Awakening to Your Life's Purpose*. New York: Penguin Group, 2005.

Tournay, Audrey and the Aspen Valley Beavers. *Beaver Tales*. Ontario: Boston Mills Press, 2003.

Turla, Peter and Hawkins, Kathleen L. *Time Management Made Easy*. New York: Penguin Books, 1994.

Vaughan, Frances and Walsh, Roger (ed.). *Accept This Gift: Selections from a Course in Miracles*. Los Angeles: Jeremy P. Tarcher, 1983.

_____. *A Gift of Peace: Selections from a Course in Miracles*. Los Angeles: Jeremy P. Tarcher, 1986.

Wakefield, Pat A. and Carrara, Larry. *A Moose for Jessica*. New York: Puffin, 1992.

Warner, Carolyn. *The Last Word: A Treasury of Women's Quotes*. Englewood Cliffs, NJ: Prentice Hall, 1992.

Whitfield, Charles. *Healing the Child Within*. Deerfield Beach, FL: Health Communications, 1987.

Wilhelm, Richard. *The I Ching (translation)*. Princeton, NJ: Princeton University Press, 1967.

Williams, Margery. *The Velveteen Rabbit*. New York: Alfred A Knopf, 1983.

Williamson, Marianne. *The Age of Wisdom: Embracing a New Midlife*. Carlsbad, CA: Hay House, 2008.

Yee, Patrick. *On Being Happy*. San Francisco: Chronicle Books, 1994.

Zander, Rosamund Stone and Zander, Benjamin. *The Art of Possibility: Transforming Professional and Personal Life*. New York: Penguin Group, 2000.

To be an actor, you have to be a child.

— Paul Newman, actor

Appendix N
Recommended Texts: Theater Books

Acting

Bates, Brian. *The Way of the Actor.* Boston: Shambhala, 1987.

Boleslavsky, Richard. *Acting: The First Six Lessons.* New York: Theater Arts Books, 1933.

Burton, Hall (ed.) *Great Acting.* New York: Bonanza Books, 1967.

Chaiken, Joseph. *The Presence of the Actor.* New York: Atheneum, 1972.

Chekhov, Michael. *To the Actor.* New York: Harper and Row, 1953.

_____. *To the Director and Playwright.* New York: Harper and Row, 1965.

_____. *Lessons For the Professional Actor.* New York: Performing Art Journal Publications, 1985.

Funke, Lewis. *Actors Talk About Acting.* Chicago: The Dramatic Publishing Company, 1977.

Hagen, Uta. *Respect for Acting.* Chicago: The Dramatic Publishing Company, 1977.

_____. *A Challenge For The Actor.* New York: Charles Scribner's Sons, 1991.

Kalter, Joan Marie. *Actors on Acting.* New York: Sterling Publishing Company, 1981.

Mekler, Eva. *The New Generation of Acting Teachers.* New York: Penguin Books, 1987.

_____. *Masters of the Stage.* New York: Grove Weindenfeld, 1989.

Oliver, Laurence. *On Acting.* New York: Simon and Schuster, 1986.

Pasoli, Robert. *A Book on the Open Theater.* New York: The Bobbs-Merrill Company, 1970.

Shurtleff, Michael. *Audition.* New York: Walker Publishing Company, Inc, 1978.

Stanislavksi, Constantin. *Building a Character.* New York: Theater Arts Books, 1949.

_____. *An Actor Prepares.* New York: Theater Arts Books, 1963.

_____. *Creating a Role.* New York: Theater Arts Books, 1965.

Strasberg, Lee. *At the Actors Studio.* New York: The Viking Press, 1965.

Movement

Alexander, Matthias F. *The Resurrection of the Body.* New York: Dell Publishing Company, 1969.

De Mille, Richard. *Put Your Mother on the Ceiling. New York:* Penguin, 1977.

Grotoski, Jerzy. *Towards a Poor Theater.* New York: Simon and Schuster, 1968.

Johnstone, Keith, *Improv.* New York: Routledge, 1981.

Pisk, Litz. *The Actor and His Body.* New York: Theater Arts Books, 1976.

Schechner, Richard. *Environmental Theater.* New York: Hawthorn Books, 1973.

Schoop, Trudi, *Won't You Join the Dance.* Palo Alto: Mayfield Publishing Company, 1974.

Shawn, Ted. *Every Little Movement.* Brooklyn: Dance Horizons, 1954.

Spolin, Viola. *Improvisation for the Theater.* Evanston, IL: Northwestern University Press, 1963.

_____. *Theater Games for the Classroom.* Evanston, IL: Northwestern University Press, 1986.

Yakim, Moni. *Creating a Character: A Physical Approach to Acting.* New York: Watson-Guptill Publications, 1990.

Speech

Berry, Cicely. *Voice and the Actor.* New York: Macmillan Publishing Company, 1973.

King, Robert G. and DiMichael, Eleanor. *Improving Articulation and Voice.* Toronto: The Macmillan Company, 1966.

Levy, Louis. Mammen, Edward W., Sonkin Robert. *Voice and Speech Handbook.* Englewood Cliffs, NJ: Prentice Hall, 1950.

Machlin, Evangeline. *Speech for the Stage.* New York: Theater Arts Books, 1966.

Linklater, Kristin. *Freeing the Natural Voice.* New York: Drama Book Specialists, 1976.

Turner, J. Clifford. *Voice and Speech in the Theater.* New York: Pitman Publishing Corporation, 1950.

Backword

Have you ever read a Backword? Creativity is about thinking out of the box. A Backword is out of the box.

A book sometimes has a Foreword. In reading a Backword, you go the other way in the book. How can that be done?

1. Open to any page.

2. Let your finger land any place on the page.

3. Do that exercise alone or with a group.

Or just read the book backwards.

What in your life can be done backwards?

Why do we think in normal conventional ways? It's safe. It's predictable. It can be boring.

To think out of the box, just like a jack-in-the-box, takes you by surprise. Creativity takes us by surprise. If we follow our hunches and nudges, we live with wonder, excitement and discovery. What could be better?

There will only be one of you in all of time. You are unique. You are special. You are creative.

And maybe this should have been the Foreword, but then I couldn't have called it a Backword.

About the Author

Jeannie Lindheim has taught acting, movement, improvisation, creativity, auditioning, and characterization techniques for thirty years at a variety of educational institutions including The Boston Conservatory, Harvard University Law School (Theater in the Courtroom), Boston University, Boston College, Lesley University's Graduate Expressive Therapies Program and others. She ran her own theater school for thirteen years. She is currently the director of Jeannie Lindheim's Center for Creativity – Turning Inspiration into Action, where she offers diverse workshops.

In 1996, she traveled to Russia with Patch Adams. Upon her return, she founded the Hearts and Noses Hospital Clown Troupe, which has since entertained over 50,000 children. After Hurricane Katrina, Jeannie went to Houston to support the New Orleans evacuees there. She spent a week at the George R. Brown Convention Center clowning and doing "by the cot" visits to 1,100 people. She has also written a unique Training Program for improvisational hospital clowning that has been sold throughout the United States as well as in twenty-three other countries (www.hospital-clowns.org).

Jeannie has conducted more than 100 regional and national workshops for primary care and specialty physician groups on Dealing with Challenging Patients and Situations, and Communicating to Patients with Life-Threatening Illnesses. She has worked with every age group and many different types of groups including teachers, theater companies, actors, sociology professors, high school principals, law students, high school dropouts, graduate and undergraduate students in education, physicians, nurses, senior citizens, teenagers, young children and people with disabilities.

Jeannie was a recipient of the 1999-2000 Boston Celtics' "Heroes Among Us" Award, in recognition of "individuals in our community who have made an overwhelming impact on the lives of others." In 2003, she was a recipient of the Exceptional Women Award sponsored by Boston's radio station Magic 106.7. In 2005, she was featured in Joanne Gordon's book, *Be Happy at Work: 100 Women Who Love Their Jobs, and Why.*

Jeannie has acted professionally and holds a Master of Arts degree in Dramatic Literature from the University of California and a Master of Fine Arts from Brandeis University. She also studied theater at the Royal Academy of Dramatic Art in London and HB Studios in New York City. She currently lives in Boston with her husband. Their children have flown the coop. Jeannie is available for keynotes and workshops.

Contact Information

Jeannie Lindheim's Center for Creativity
P.O. Box 471025
Brookline, MA 02447
jeannie@center4creativity.org

www.center4creativity.org § www.trustingthemoment.com